THE
CATHOLIC
CAMPUS

THE
CATHOLIC
CAMPUS

Edward Wakin

THE MACMILLAN COMPANY, NEW YORK

COLLIER-MACMILLAN LTD., LONDON

First Printing

The Macmillan Company, New York
Collier-Macmillan Canada Limited, Galt, Ontario
Divisions of The Crowell-Collier Publishing Company

Printed in the United States of America

Library of Congress catalog card number: 63-11811

DESIGNED BY JOAN LAWS

Some of the material in this book originally appeared in a slightly different form in The Sign. *The Preface appeared in the* Fordham Alumni *magazine.*

To Daniel Joseph

PREFACE

THE university is a phenomenon quite Catholic in its origins and significance. In her long history as creator and nourisher of social institutions, the Church has not been a very frequent borrower. Her first social organization was a close imitation of the legal structure of the Roman Empire—the diocese. This was and still is the basic organizational unity of the Church. As time is reckoned from Rome, her first great social addition to this basic pattern followed swiftly. This was the monastery. And with about the same lapse of time the monastery itself, in conjunction with the diocese, gave birth to the university. It is easy to describe these great creations in terms of facultative psychology as the hands, heart and head of the Church. But leaving aside the satisfaction we might derive from metaphor, one thing is true: the removal of any one of these three basic institutions would mean the Church would not be fully itself. This calls for a close look at the university.

The vision of what a university does begins quite simply with a clear perception of what man is—what constitutes true human dignity. And man is most basically, most importantly, a knowing and a choosing creature. These are his highest activities, his greatest glory. True human dignity consists of growth in these—growth in knowledge and growth in virtue. Other skills, other achievements can smooth his way. These alone can make him more fully man. The university's role is to foster this essential human growth broadly and deeply—through a group of faculties for conserving, disseminating and advancing all possible learning. In time the word "university" has taken on various shades of meaning, but it still stands, at least, for some true breadth of educational horizon. For its faculty and for its students, the university endeavors to provide the three-dimensional perspective of full human living.

No university can achieve this breadth of vision without a restless, hungry, goading quest for quality. There must be a quest for quality of educational purpose in every program; for quality in professional faculty growth at every level; for quality in the techniques and the tools of teaching; for quality in choice of students—seeking those who can achieve what the university stands for and then challenging, stimulating, intellectually disciplining them to the utmost of their individual capabilities.

And it is in this pursuit of quality in the fostering of true human growth that the university basically and essentially serves its community. There is an urgency today as never before to this unremitting quest: for upon it depends survival in our nuclear age. We have left the pioneer days when brawn and courage and human prudence and goodwill were enough to build a brave new world and defend it. Today, widespread theoretical and

technical knowledge is necessary merely to prevent society's collapse from its own complexity. Only through
the dedicated pursuit of quality in its total endeavor can
the university give to today's youth the breadth and
clarity of vision they will need for the sake of all of us
in tomorrow's world.

In the order of practical reality, of course, no university of our day can encompass all fields of knowledge.
Our duty is to seek out the specific task and destiny of
the Catholic university in a pluralistic society and then
endeavor to achieve it with all our energies.

Theologically, it is the destiny of the Catholic university to bear witness to the Incarnation of the Son of
God. Despite the many other needs of the Church and
the heavy financial burden a university imposes and the
relatively small percentage of Catholic youth who can
actually attend it, the destiny of the Catholic university
in itself is its own justification. It stands there as a sign,
a sign that the Son of God really entered our human
history and that in so doing He sanctified all truth, the
truth of science as well as the truth of Scripture, the
truth of technology as well as that of tradition. Theologically, the university gives proof that the Church is
concerned with the totality of human living.

Educationally, the Catholic university makes its specific contribution to society in two ways: in breadth,
by including theology in the core of its programs of
study; in depth, by adding another dimension to all knowing—the spiritual implications for thought and for act
in every phase of human life.

The world needs the specific contributions a Catholic

university can make today. It presents, almost uniquely, an ordered vision of reality—humanities, science, philosophy, theology. By showing the way to a hierarchy of values and a unity of purpose based on philosophical principles, it effects some harmony in the tensions that sunder modern man. And most basically of all: since in life or in a university one cannot with impunity isolate himself from reality and the absolute reality of God is the structuring principle of all other realities, the Catholic university is uniquely destined for the fulfillment of human personality by providing the vision of this ultimate divine reality.

As with a man, so with a university, to live fully implies an awareness not only of the roots of our own human past, of the vistas of our future divine destiny, but also of our brothers who walk beside us in this present time and in this place. We are of the here and the now and responsible for the world about us.

One specific and essential contribution to our contemporary way of life, which it is the destiny of the Catholic university to make, I would call "the courage of commitment." It has been said well that the tragedy of the struggle in our day is that it is between those who believe and care very much and those who so lack belief they cannot care. The worship of the uncommitted mind, for which all truth is relative, has led only too facilely to the decadence of the uncommitted heart which can find no loyalty worth its choosing. For the builders and the planners and the leaders of the Catholic university this is not so. For them, truth is and the mind can know at least some part of it. For them, the good is and the will can choose at least some measure of it. For them, this is what it means to be a man, this courage of commitment, this way of life.

The Catholic university brings a sense of tradition, of roots to a pluralistic society too easily lost and rootless. It brings a sense of unity that does not crush diversity, of harmony that does not impose uniformity. It brings a humanistic mental attitude to a scientifically preoccupied unsmiling world. But above all, I think, by exemplifying the fact and therefore the possibility of full intellectual, spiritual commitment, it brings to a nearly discouraged world an awareness that there are things worth caring for in life—some of them more than life itself.

It is a simple fact that the life and spirit of Catholic education is not sufficiently understood or appreciated in academic America. When Fordham underwent the rigorous examination that preceded the awarding of its Phi Beta Kappa Chapter, it was evident that the men of obvious goodwill and academic prominence who came to look at us felt as though they were embarking on strange seas indeed, where all sorts of monsters might lie in wait for the unwary intellectual explorer. That they found neither monsters nor distortion of value is a tribute to all of Fordham's faculty and administrators. But that, in coming to us, they were not quite sure what to expect, is perhaps the clearest indication of the vast job that still lies ahead for all Catholic colleges and universities.

Because of this lagging knowledge of Catholic higher education, it is a matter of personal pleasure that a member of our Fordham faculty has undertaken the task of describing a representative sample of Catholic colleges and universities. He approaches these institutions—as he should—as an independent observer presenting a carefully prepared report on the extent, variety and values of Catholic higher education in America.

Laurence J. McGinley, S.J.
President, Fordham University

CONTENTS

Preface by Laurence J. McGinley, S.J.   vii

Introduction: Colleges with a View   1

1. The Catholic University of America
    The Scope is Catholic   11

2. University of Notre Dame
    The Will to Win   33

3. St. Louis University
    "Ratio Studiorum" on the Mississippi   69

4. Rosary College
    Beauty and the Books   96

5. St. John's, Collegeville
    Living Life Whole   113

6. Marymount College of Virginia
   An Invitation to Learn   133

7. Marillac College
   Only Nuns Need Apply   149

8. Rosary Hill
   The Creation of a College   167

9. The Changing Catholic Campus   193

THE
CATHOLIC
CAMPUS

INTRODUCTION

Colleges with a View

THE WALLS around the
Catholic campus have come tumbling down since the
end of World War II. As a generalization this has notable
exceptions, but it does epitomize the postwar transformation of Catholic colleges and universities. In outlook
and in actual operations, in quantity and in quality, Catholic higher education has emerged as an important enterprise in the mainstream of American higher education.

By the 1960's, Catholic colleges and universities constituted a nationwide network of higher education, enrolling one-third of a million students in 238 institutions.
The expansion of the 1950's will carry forward into the
decade ahead with ambitious plans to build, improve and

1

expand further as Catholic schools evaluate themselves, not just against each other, but against all American schools. In a 1962 compilation of long-range fund-raising campaigns exceeding $10,000,000, the American Association of Fund Raising Counsel listed a total of $575 million being raised by Catholic colleges and universities. These millions will not only be used for bricks and mortar, but also in the three areas where Catholic schools are trying to catch up with their secular counterparts: faculty salaries, student scholarships, and endowment funds.

Catholic higher education in the United States is largely a twentieth century development, the uppermost level of learning in the world's largest private school system. It is a system built in a hurry by the American Catholic Church, which until 1908 was still regarded by the Vatican as a missionary church. Though Catholic higher education in the New World dates from 1789 when Georgetown University was founded, more than two-thirds of the 238 Catholic colleges and universities have been founded in this century. There are also 39 diocesan teachers colleges and teacher-training institutions, practically all of them founded in the postwar period, enrolling 4,000 men and women religious.

Generally speaking, the first half of the century was the seeding time. In 1900, there were only 70 Catholic colleges. Enrollment in 1908 was 16,000, a figure that rose steadily, except for a slowdown in the early depression thirties, until it reached 103,000 in 1940, a total that was dwarfed by the abrupt postwar breakthrough. The 1961 enrollment of 326,000 regular students was three times as great, a figure that excludes summer, special and adult education students.

As might be expected, the largest Catholic universities have developed in the big cities where large numbers of Catholic immigrants settled. According to figures compiled in October, 1961, by the Department of Education of the National Catholic Welfare Conference, these include Marquette with about 12,000 students; Detroit University and St. John's University in Brooklyn, slightly under 11,000 each; Fordham University, almost 10,000; Loyola (Chicago) and Seton Hall Universities, about 9,300 each. While women's religious orders have founded smaller colleges than the men's orders, they have founded many more of them, 146 of the 238. The largest women's colleges, with enrollments of about 1,300, are Mount Mercy (Pittsburgh), the College of St. Rose (Albany, New York) and the College of St. Catherine (St. Paul).

Geographically, Chicago can be taken as the center of a circle with a 500-mile radius that would enclose a large part of the Catholic college and university enrollment. Nationally, the 25 largest institutions enroll about half the Catholic total; the substantial majority attend coeducational institutions. The Jesuits have the largest single stake, with 28 schools that include every major city (except Pittsburgh) and contain about one-third of the total enrollment.

Unlike Catholic elementary and high schools, the Catholic college was never an official American Catholic project. Each college arose as a distinctive response to a variety of local situations, drawing on available resources and depending on the initiative of a variety of religious

orders. While Catholic higher education may look monolithic to the outsider, to the insider it often seems
chaotic. A mosaic is more accurate, and that is why the
Catholic campus story must be told by a diversified sample of schools reflecting its variety as well as its progress
and problems. While the ensuing profiles of eight institutions are intended to be sympathetic and construc-
tive, they are also uninhibited. They include material
that will not be found in a college catalog, a president's
report or a fund-raiser's brochure. Postwar Catholic
higher education has moved beyond the pious panegyric.

Each institution where this writer explored campus
life and talked endlessly to students, faculty members
and administrators was a fascinating and self-centered
world in itself. Self-centeredness is part of any college
campus where the central reality is the school itself, a
subject which draws out everyone—from student newspaper editor to president, from cafeteria waiter to the
dean of men. Only on leaving is it possible to view a
campus in perspective, for it envelops even the onlooker;
only in retrospect do its passing tempests, local issues,
and inflated self-image assume proper proportions.

Because the nucleus of a Catholic campus is a religious
order and, almost invariably, a surrounding circle of
graduates who have returned as professors, it is a composite of many life stories. This is the case more than on
a secular campus, since a man's faith, as well as his work,
is involved. For Catholic laymen and priests or religious,
their Catholic campus is the framework for their lives,
their vocations, their ideals, their religious commitment.
They have watched economic boom and bust, war and

peace, the death of presidents and popes and the election of new ones from within the context of their academic home. Their college becomes superimposed over professional careers, life experiences, involvement with nation and with church. Many a layman, priest or religious grows old in this academic world, his personality and his self inextricably blended into one particular Catholic campus.

While bishops, diocesan priests and religious orders control or govern all Catholic colleges and universities, the layman carries on most of the teaching responsibilities. His predominance surprises outsiders. Though in some schools the religious are in the majority, in many schools, particularly the larger universities, students may encounter priests or religious only in philosophy and religion courses. On a nationwide basis, the lay faculty members outnumber priests and religious by two to one. Out of 25,500 full-time faculty members, more than 14,000 are laymen, 3,100 women. The remaining places are filled by 4,200 nuns, 3,700 priests and about 400 brothers. Moreover, many on the lay faculty are not Catholics, and their numbers are increasing. By contrast, in 1940 laymen and women constituted half of a nationwide total of 13,142 faculty members in 193 Catholic institutions.

When the faculty members of a major Catholic university were polled on the status of Catholic universities, 64 percent felt that Catholic institutions are not accepted by other colleges and universities as having an equal place in higher education. Eighty-five percent felt that the general public is not aware of the extent and accomplishments of Catholic higher education. Part of the ex-

planation is the lag between the postwar emergence of
Catholic institutions and general awareness of this development.

The situation is also complicated by an Ivy League
fixation on one hand and a defensive mentality on the
other. The tendency to compare newly emerging Catholic schools with the handful of American schools of
Ivy League caliber is unrealistic, even though a few
Catholic educators provoke such comparisons. In fact,
not many of America's 2,000 institutions of higher learning can bear such comparisons. Moreover, the great academic reputations are made on the graduate level where
Catholic higher education is still breaking ground.

A few Catholic educators with a defensive mentality
tend to ignore present problems and past shortcomings.
Prewar Catholic higher education left much to be de-
sired. In fact, leading Catholic educators will admit pri-
vately that, overall, it could not be taken seriously. Msgr.
James M. Campbell, Dean of Catholic University's College of Arts and Sciences for the past thirty years, wrote
in 1939: "I do not believe that anyone in a position to
know all the facts will find the following statements on
the American Catholic college unjust: that no more
than a dozen Catholic colleges in this country are as
good academically as the better non-Catholic institutions;
that of these dozen almost all are colleges for women."
Looking back over that prewar situation, a foremost leader in Catholic higher education added a double
postscript: "Possibly that was all we could expect under
the circumstances and, also, there was awareness of the
need to improve."

The current quality of Catholic higher education is appropriately discussed in terms of recent developments and in relation to the "better non-Catholic institutions." By contrast with the past, favorable postwar generalizations would be accepted by non-Catholic as well as Catholic educators. Accreditation by regional asociations is so widespread that it can be taken for granted as a minimum achievement by Catholic schools. In a report published in 1960, it was found that 87 percent of four-year Catholic colleges and universities had met the standards and requirements of their regional accrediting organizations. This compared with 73 percent of Protestant and 41 percent of all other private institutions.

Only recently have Catholic schools pursued the prestige labels of Phi Beta Kappa, Rhodes Scholarships and Woodrow Wilson Fellowships, among others. So far, there are only three Catholic campuses awarding Phi Beta Kappa keys, compared to 167 secular institutions, but Catholic educators are actively pursuing acceptance, a long, tedious, bureaucratic process. In recent years, Catholic schools have begun to make a showing in the competition for Rhodes Scholarships. One notable example is Fordham, which did not have a Rhodes scholar until 1960; the following year it had two more. In the first forty years of the Rhodes program, Catholic schools won only five scholarships, but in the fifteen years between 1946 and 1962, they won ten, twice as many. Notre Dame, with five, has had the greatest number. While fifteen remains an unimpressive total out of 1,670 Rhodes Scholarships awarded, the postwar improvement is a clue to the progress on the Catholic campus.

In the competition for Woodrow Wilson Fellowships, awarded since the end of World War II to prospective professors, the performance of the Catholic college has been noteworthy. Notre Dame, St. Louis and Fordham, which have had the most winners, rank above or close to the prestige secular universities in their regions. This, rather than an Ivy League comparison, would seem to be the most realistic. Notre Dame, with 78 winners as of the 1961–1962 school year, compares with Northwestern, 47, and Chicago, 77. St. Louis, with 36, compares with Washington University, 41, and the University of Missouri, 40. Fordham, with 28, has four more than its traditional athletic rival, New York University. While it is misleading to count scholarships and fellowships as if they were touchdowns, the underlying point remains that Catholic higher education has moved ahead dramatically in the postwar period, comparing favorably with its regional counterparts in the secular field. Nonetheless, no responsible educator sees a Catholic Harvard on the horizon.

With all this in mind, the following eight profiles of the Catholic campus begin with Catholic University, a proper starting point because of its strategic position in Catholic higher education. It is also unique. Unlike any other Catholic institution, it is primarily a graduate school and it is an official project of the American Catholic Church. But it is also a microcosm of the Catholic effort in higher education. On the other hand, Notre Dame, the best known Catholic institution, is probably the most misrepresented and the most controversial. St. Louis University, large, urban, and coed, personifies the Jesuit penchant for the teeming city and the ambitious academic enterprise. Rosary College, a strong liberal arts school, is suburban (outside Chicago) and for women only; St. John's, Collegeville, Minnesota, is rural, isolated, for men only.

Three postwar schools are included, each for different reasons. Marymount College of Virginia represents a venture into the area of junior colleges which are emerging as a new force in higher education. Marillac College, for nuns only, is a dramatic manifestation of the Sister Formation Movement, which the Catholic sociologist Thomas F. O'Dea has called "one of the most significant educational developments within contemporary American Catholicism." Rosary Hill College in Buffalo, New York, symbolizes the college-founding propensities of women's religious orders at their best.

In one way or another, these eight schools reflect the variety of the Catholic campus, much of its personality dependent on physical setting and local conditions. Also represented are varying styles of Catholic religious orders, ranging from the Holy Cross Fathers of Notre Dame with their strong institutional pride to the Benedictines at St. John's who shy from institutional pride. There are the Jesuits who tend to think first as Jesuits, then in terms of their institutions, usually urban, while the Benedictines with their vow of stability, stay fixed in place, pursuing an intellectual and spiritual totality, usually in a rural setting. At Rosary College, the Dominicans demonstrate their tradition of intellectuality; at Rosary Hill, the Franciscans their stress on harmony in personal relations.

Each Catholic campus reflects the influence of its religious order as well as its environment, its student body, and its academic aims. The sum total of the eight institutions pictured here is, hopefully, a miniature mosaic of 238 institutions, each different after its fashion, each fundamentally the same in its Catholic commitment. With all their variety, they remain colleges with a view.

THE CATHOLIC UNIVERSITY
OF AMERICA

The Scope Is Catholic

PROBABLY on no other campus in America are the sacred and the secular, the mediaeval and the modern, the canon lawyer and the coed, the Thomistic philosopher and the nuclear physicist blended in such surprising juxtaposition as at The Catholic University of America in Washington, D.C. Because members of 87 religious communities live nearby and study there, the University area is referred to as "little Rome." Because it has educated so many bishops, monsignori and priests in important positions, it is often known as a "West Point for United States clergy." It

11

is clearly the Establishment University for American Catholicism.

But the University has a strong aversion to the misnomer, "superseminary," sometimes applied to it. There are three times as many laymen and women as priests and religious in its student body and on its faculty. As one professor remarked, "Have you ever seen a seminary with a nuclear reactor on the lawn and a squad of coed cheerleaders practicing in the gym?"

Placed at the pinnacle of Catholic education in this country when it opened on November 13, 1889, Catholic University is under the direct and "full jurisdiction" of the United States Bishops and subject directly to the Sacred Congregation of Seminaries and Universities in the Vatican. Its future development was foreshadowed in 1866 when United States Bishops at the Second Plenary Council of Baltimore announced their intention to found a Catholic university "in which all branches of literature and science, both sacred and profane, should be taught." The seed that was planted with a School of Sacred Sciences (now called the School of Sacred Theology) has produced a university with so many branches of learning that it is the colossus of graduate training among Catholic institutions. Catholic University is, in fact, primarily a graduate school with a growing undergraduate college which was not part of the founders' original intention. Its rector, the Rt. Rev. William J. McDonald, describes Catholic University as "the Catholic Church in action in the field of learning." It is the appropriate place to begin a report on the Catholic campus in the United States.

On a single Wednesday afternoon—the first day of a visit to Catholic University—the campus was a microcosm of Catholic higher education from coast to coast. Indeed, the university's range, variety and far-reaching research were a surprise, its campus juxtapositions immediately obvious. In Room 21 of the Music Building, students in Speech and Drama 302, "Theory and Technique of Acting," sat around discussing reading assignments and praising the performance of a Jesuit who had played God in a theatrical production. Then the lay professor arrived, opened the class with a prayer and launched into a stimulating lecture on how an actor arrives at understanding of the character he is playing. Toward the end of class, a blonde coed was called upon to demonstrate her interpretation of Blanche in Tennessee Williams' play, *A Streetcar Named Desire.* She sat on a desk, pursed her lips, crossed her legs, and prepared to capture the mood of that troubled Southern lady, whose line at the moment was, "I know what it's like to be lonely." A short time before, a class of priests in a building nearby heard a lecture delivered in Latin on dogmatic theology. Their second semester subject matter was *"de peccato originali; de novissimis."*

On the other end of the campus, several physics students worked on an experiment in centrifugal force, while in the new Engineering and Architecture Building the nuclear reactor was being prepared to raise controlled havoc with the atom. On that same afternoon, the dog-eared Class Schedule which had been loaned to this visitor listed a bewildering range of class lectures. A random sample: Biblical Greek, Introduction to Personal Counseling, Romantic Period in Music, Operating Room Nursing, Aircraft Design, Europe Since 1914, Climatology, Elizabethan Drama, Microwave Generation.

Later that same Wednesday, meetings were held by the graduate women's sodality, the track club, Kappa Tau Gamma sorority, Phi Kappa Theta fraternity, the Pan American Club, the Cardinal Charities Committee and the marriage forum. In McMahon Hall, the academic mood was being shattered by a rehearsal for the campus variety show. According to the script, it was Easter vacation in the West Indies and a disheveled chorus line of coeds in slacks, skirts, and sweat shirts was belting out the line: "We're going to meet all the men we can."

It was a day like any other at Catholic University, where simplified descriptions totter and fall because of the size of its commitment to Catholicism, America, and higher learning. Forty-two buildings on 140 acres in northeast Washington are a small container for the large role which C.U. aims at filling. According to its statutes: "The aim of The Catholic University of America is to search out truth scientifically, to safeguard it, and to apply it to the moulding and shaping of both private and public life. With this aim in view the University imparts, carefully cultivates and promotes learning, and furnishes both students and teachers with the means for scientific research and study, and so directs them that they may properly fulfil their duties toward God, Church and Country. The University must look to the welfare not only of the students enrolled but also of all the faithful in the United States of America, and hence it should be of help and assistance to schools, colleges and seminaries, especially by training teachers who shall be qualified to instruct Catholic youth in these institutions. Thus the University should be a national center of Catholic culture, and should be held as such by all."

The University's commitment to higher learning is personified by its student body of 4,645. The graduate students (currently 55 percent of the total) are always in the majority, unlike any other Catholic university. Some campus traditionalists—unrealistically—would like C.U. to abandon undergraduate training altogether, but this is a minority opinion. "Catholic University's reason for existing is found on the graduate level," a long-time member of the faculty pointed out. "Anything on the undergraduate level can be duplicated in most other Catholic schools. We are trying to educate not leaders, but leaders of leaders; for instance the professors who will train others at Catholic colleges or the priests who fill key positions in chanceries throughout the U.S."

The graduate-school emphasis was reflected in a nationwide study which showed that C.U. granted 543 doctorates in the arts, humanities, and social sciences between 1936 and 1950, thirteenth in the country. This total was only slightly less than the grand total for all the other 14 Catholic institutions covered in the study. The figure of 543, incidentally, does not include the hundreds of doctorates awarded in Sacred Theology and Canon Law. At the 1962 graduation exercises, 71 percent of the 1,205 degrees awarded were for graduate work.

The Schools of Philosophy, Canon Law and Sacred Theology are unique in this country; the latter two, where Latin is the classroom language, account for the University's designation as a "West Point for U.S. clergy." The School of Sacred Theology is a clerical melting pot, enrolling 151 students from 31 different religious communities and 133 seminarians from 49 U.S. dioceses. While practically all the faculty members in the three schools are priests, one of the most renowned is a layman who converted from Judaism. He is the canon lawyer, Professor Stephan Kuttner.

On the other hand, the Graduate School of Arts and Sciences has 1,570 students in 21 departments, but only 466 of them are priests, brothers or nuns. Its overwhelmingly lay faculty has a wide range of backgrounds and is the pride of C.U. It maintains an impressive record of scholarly output, which in some fields has often stressed so-called "Catholic" subjects. Insofar as this is the case, its impact on the wider academic community of American higher education has been limited. Comparing the graduate school before and after World War II, a leading faculty member recalled that when he arrived in the 1930's there were only "a few good departments." "Now," he added, "it is a university in every sense of the word." Although singling out any department is difficult, a list of the most renowned must include the departments of speech and drama, sociology, Semitic languages, history, and physics.

The C.U. faculty tries to maintain a balanced pattern of both research and teaching, though many faculty members find their campus duties leave them too little time for research. The University also needs more graduate fellowships so it can bid for top students everywhere

in the country; at the moment most full-time graduate
students come from Catholic colleges in the East. Comparing his present department with a secular one in
which he taught previously, a professor in the graduate
school said: "We have a much better community feeling, and the students maintain a generally higher level,
though we don't have the handful of excessively brilliant students."

In addition to the Graduate School of Arts and Sciences, students pursuing masters' degrees and doctorates
are in the School of Engineering and Architecture, the
School of Nursing and the National Catholic School of
Social Service. In the areas staked out by each of these
arms of the University, the continuous demand for their
graduates testifies to their reputations, and in the course
of a visit to C.U., all are likely to be pointed to with
pride. Off campus, there is the University's Columbus
School of Law, the result of a 1954 merger with the
Law School of Columbus University. A charter and
only Catholic member of the Association of American
Universities, Catholic University is also one of only
three Catholic colleges empowered to award a Phi Beta
Kappa key. (The others are the College of St. Catherine
in St. Paul and, since 1962, Fordham.)

On campus, the graduate students, many of them
attending on a part-time basis, seem to be in hiding.
Wrapped in their specialties and departmental requirements, they must be ferreted out of library alcoves or
basement laboratories. They live on tight little islands
of research and study, surrounded by the highly visible
undergraduate minority. Together, undergraduate and

graduate students are an image-maker's nightmare; they make it impossible to talk of the typical C.U. student or of a C.U. image. Academically, their pursuit of studies is as varied as the University curriculum; geographically, they come from all 50 states and 60 foreign countries; socially, they range from the fraternity or sorority president to the nun who must go directly from class to her order's house of study. They include the religious who arrive by "school buses" plying a regular route between outlying residences and the doorstep of John K. Mullen Memorial Library and the coed who sits in class taking notes, a basketball player on one side, a St. Joseph nun on the other.

In daylight, the campus is a mosaic of religious, priests, coeds, and college boys. The atmosphere is more like that of a small college than a high-powered university; it is friendly, casual, subdued. Though the students joke about the rector's favorite phrase, "our University family," they seem to feel that it is an apt description. On the student level, not much is made of the difference between the lay and the religious. This is occasionally underlined by campus remarks and student hijinks, including one April Fool's issue of the school paper that unnerved the administration. A magisterial nun on the faculty was pictured on the newspaper's front page in a football uniform.

C.U. coeds are fond of remarking, "Why do all the cute boys wear their collars turned around?" According to student informants, the Xaverian Brother is regarded as the Joe College of the religious; five years running, the Xaverian Brothers won the basketball league for seminarians and religious. While most houses of study run by the religious orders maintain files of past exams (shades of the fraternity house), it is reliably reported that the Christian Brothers have the best files of all. One professor, in announcing his policy on examinations, said his goal was: "Beat the files." A more realistic professor observed that if the students study the material covered in the exams of past years they are actually "beating" themselves. It amounts to a comprehensive review of the subject matter and also prods the professor into devising difficult questions.

While other Catholic colleges and universities in the U.S. are dominated by the personality of the single religious order owning and operating them, C.U. is a composite of many orders, an amalgam of different personalities. Nonetheless, it does have a recognizable atmosphere and a shared attitude, which might elude the outsider if it weren't for the undergraduates—impressionable, vocal and uninhibited. They convince the outsider that the threefold commitment to Church, nation and higher learning engrosses even freshmen, only a few months out of high school. As undergraduates, the students seem more serious, more mature and more committed than the stereotyped collegian. They can use such phrases as "saving our souls" without being self-conscious. They talk freely about their responsibilities as Catholics and Americans. They answer the phone in the dormitory and say, "Jim has gone to Mass" as naturally as students elsewhere might say, "Jim has gone to the movies." Though even attendance at Sunday Mass is not supervised, a large number of students go to daily

Mass. A member of the School of Sacred Theology estimated that about two hundred Masses are said daily on campus, not including those in the surrounding houses of study.

The unsilent minority of undergraduates has a sense of belonging at C.U. and when they complain they are convinced the University administration will listen. One sign of give-and-take with authority is the characteristic student grumbling about campus food (which, incidentally, failed to offend this alien palate). The administration responded by setting up a Food Committee as a forum for all levels of student gourmets. According to one issue of *Tower*, the student newspaper: "Currently being investigated is the grilled cheese sandwich 'problem.' Campus chefs hope to have an arrangement whereby the sandwiches can be taken directly from the grill to the plate. The sponge-like quality of the pancakes also came up for debate."

In a private comparison with 40 other Catholic colleges and universities, C.U. discovered that its regulations are the most liberal. There are no supervised study hours, no lights out in the dorms, not even weekday curfews for the senior men. The curfews for other students are also liberal when matched with the general practice. As Dean of Men, James J. McPadden, explains, the stress is on "self-discipline," and the system works. As confirmation, Dean McPadden, the first layman in the disciplinary post, is one of the most popular figures on the C.U. campus.

Though the United States Congress and the heart of the capital are only a short bus ride away, student life centers on the campus and the surrounding residential area of Brookland. Twelfth Street, a humdrum street of stores, is a ten-minute walk from the University where the students find—all lined up—bank, bakery, supermarket, five-and-ten, laundry, dry cleaner, People's Drug Store and Hap's (for a bottle of beer). At the Horizon bookstore, book buying ran to form, with Merton, Maritain and Gilson doing well, along with John Courtney Murray, Graham Greene and C. S. Lewis. The men preferred history, especially World War II, and the coeds fiction, particularly *To Kill a Mockingbird*, Flannery O'Connor's *A Good Man Is Hard to Find*, and *Mr. Blue*, the story of a modern-day St. Francis of Assisi. All books on the Kennedys sold well, reflecting not only the Catholic interest but also the pro-Democratic campus mood. One book was in particular demand: *Winnie Ille Pu* (the Latin version of *Winnie the Pooh*).

The college coed is a comparatively new trauma for C.U. She was not in the college before the war, but arrived in 1945 when forty-six women entered as freshmen. In 1962 there were 682 women among the 2,088 undergraduates. However, a few die-hard professors complain about "trying to teach women." One administrator reports that he is still stopped by a certain faculty member who grumbles: "Don't you think for a moment that *they* are here to stay."

There is no substitute for the sound of students talking about themselves, their goals, their college, and the C.U. students give a good account of themselves, illustrated by the following discussion that took place one afternoon in the student lounge:

FIRST FRESHMAN: "I visited several campuses in picking a college and academically they all seemed about the same. Each had its strong points. But the spirit on this campus, the attitude of the administration toward the students, provided—I felt—the most opportunity to develop into a mature man, a Christian gentleman if you want to use that phrase. . . . Even though I made only the one visit before coming here, I felt I found out a great deal from reading the propaganda—if you want to call it that—and from talking to the students. The attitude of the students and the stated attitude of the administration were at least quite a bit different from those of the other institutions. My major disappointment when I came here was the fact that not as many students as I expected took advantage of this atmosphere."

SENIOR COED: "I think a lot of the things good about C.U. are what it doesn't do. I went during my first year to a girls' school and the constant talk was, you are a . . . girl. It was an exterior development. If you had this superficial development, then it was pretty much left to yourself what you were inside. If you attended the ceremonies and were a good child and got to meals on time, brushed your teeth, got up when you were told, and did what you were told, people considered that you weren't a problem. It didn't matter whether you were thinking intelligently or acting intelligently. It just mattered that you had a nice exterior. They had decided what kind of people they wanted to turn out and they tried to put this mold on everybody. You were expected to give up your individuality and conform to this."

JUNIOR: "I feel what we're talking about is the lack of enforced regulation. Enforced Mass, enforced study hours are not used on this campus. No lights out or anything like that. During the week, there is an eleven-o'clock curfew for freshmen, midnight for sophomores and juniors, but seniors don't have any curfew."

FIRST FRESHMAN: "I think it makes a great deal of difference coming here. It sounds a little tight, but it's true. You're getting a chance to develop your whole self and a great part of this is your spiritual self. Without a realization of why you are here and what you are doing here, you can't be a full man."

SECOND FRESHMAN: "If you want to know my personal goal, it is to go to graduate school. I would like to get into politics in some way and, through that, more or less to take up my share in fighting this terrible thing called Communism. This has been with me since my last year in high school; being at C.U. has helped to make this even a bigger thing than it was before. Being here just a couple of months, I find I am more aware of what is going on around me."

JUNIOR: "My personal aims are not as political. Since coming to the university, I have become more aware of the service that Catholic college students owe to the world or at least to the United States. I would like to get into something like social work or government work where I could work with people and make my contribution to society. . . . Is this typical here? The typical C.U. man doesn't exist."

FIRST FRESHMAN: "That's the thing about this place.

There is no type in freshman year or in senior and I know quite a few graduate students. There is no C.U. type in the graduate school either."

JUNIOR: "That's one of the tremendous things about this school. You can learn from each one of these different types; each one has something to contribute."

SENIOR COED: "Though I think I can recognize any C.U. graduate. They do get a solid inner core of philosophy that a lot of people don't get."

JUNIOR: "I feel that the student is allowed to strengthen his own principles and evaluate them. It is hard to put into words, but I think what is learned in the classroom in this respect is a solidifying force for a person's principles. When you get into the outside world, there will be a majority of non-Catholics that you will be able to stand up to on your own two feet and maintain these principles, and perhaps even spread the faith upon which these principles are based."

SENIOR COED: "I think that one thing here is that the religious principles are given to you with a firm intellectual basis. You are never handed anything and told this is a matter of faith, accept it. If anyone just says that the reason he believes anything is faith, they look at him as if he is losing his grip. You are expected to have thought these things through and to have made some sort of intellectual judgment."

The C.U. attitude was also expressed by one of its most brilliant graduates of recent years, William J. Thaler, who received his doctorate in physics in 1951. He married a coed he met at the University and went directly to work for the Office of Naval Research, where he soon rose to head of the Fields Projects Branch. *The New York Times* Sunday Magazine, in an article describing him as "Down-to-Earth Wizard of Outer Space," asked why he didn't double his government salary by going into private industry. Thaler's reply: "Frankly, from a personal standpoint, making money is secondary. The thing is what I have done with myself, intellectually, spiritually, and philosophically and not what I have done materialistically. I take my religion seriously (he is a Roman Catholic) and that helps. Making money is not synonymous with success, to my mind."

On campus, the University elite—whether student or professor—combine piety, philosophical outlook and intellectual achievement. While the campus is conscious of the lay faculty members who attend daily Mass, this does not guarantee approval of their scholarship. One leading faculty member in praising the teaching contribution of a colleague and noting his attendance at daily Mass, added: "But his published works are full of mistakes. It's a disgrace." From the University's rector to the editor of the college paper, one theme recurs: Good Catholics are not necessarily good scholars and vice versa. The rector, in stressing the importance of intellectual achievement, pointed out, "Only when we have both clergy and laity who are competent in their fields will we have books and texts that breathe the Christian spirit." The University's attitude is that Christianity and scholarship are not only compatible but inseparable.

This attitude is exemplified in all areas from the class in acting, in which a coed played a character from Tennesee Williams, to the boundaries of theoretical physics. The professor in the dramatics class noted that in discussing various plays, man's moral responsibility provides a framework in which the characters play out their parts. "In playing an evil character," he said, "the actor should not interject his own judgment that the character is bad. Play the character as intended by the author and his evil will come through. For instance, there is no mistaking the evil in Iago." Dr. Karl Herzfeld, the renowned chairman of the Physics Department, exemplifies the sense of unity sought at C.U. Every morning he can be seen assisting at Mass, in the afternoon at his desk facing a blackboard full of undecipherable chalk marks that are meaningful to the nuclear physicist, and in the evening relating physics to philosophy. His characteristic remark in a lecture that was later published has the sound of C.U.: "On the whole, I think modern physics is closer to scholastic philosophy than was nineteenth century physics, for several reasons. . . ."

In that vast intellectual area this side of heresy, the faculty members feel that the University has had a strong tradition of academic freedom and that they can sometimes handle subject matter with more freedom than, for instance, professors in state universities. One philosophy professor pointed out that Thomistic philosophy is required, "but a student can reject it and still pass." He passes not because he believes it, "but because he really knows it." Everywhere you turn, a monolithic image of C.U. becomes a mirage; there are too many different academic disciplines and personalities involved, too many religious orders, too many scholars with varied backgrounds. A professor is hired for his scholarship and that includes the non-Catholics on the faculty. Even in the School of Sacred Theology, a faculty member reminded the visitor, "There is more than one opinion possible on many questions of theology, though many people on the outside regard theology as a closed book."

From all indications, C.U. seems to have a devoted faculty, which goes about its work convinced in most cases that the school's administration is on its side. Generally, C.U. has no turnover problem, except in those instances where business and government lure away members. But it does have a problem recruiting faculty, though recent salary increases have made the school more competitive on this score.

At the beginning of each scholastic year, the Catholic members of the faculty attend the Mass of the Holy Spirit at which they make the Profession of Faith and take the Oath Against Modernism, which are required of faculties in pontifical institutions. The Modernism Oath begins with these words, "I firmly accept and hold all that is defined, laid down, and declared by the unerring teaching authority of the Church, especially those points of doctrine which are directly opposed to the errors of the present time." Also included in the Oath is the revealing statement: "I likewise condemn and reject the opinion of those who hold that the more intelligent Christian man may have, as it were, a double personality, one as a believer and the other as an historian, as though he could hold as an historian things contradictory to his faith as a believer or could lay down premises from which it would follow that certain doctrines were either false or doubtful, provided he did not directly deny the doctrines themselves." On modernism, "I declare myself entirely opposed to that error taught by those modernists who claim there is nothing divine in sacred tradition or, what is far worse, who admit the divine in a pantheistic sense, so that there remains nothing but this simple, bare fact to be accommodated to the facts of history, that men by their own industry, ingenuity, and skill have kept up through the ages the school of thought begun by Christ and the Apostles." While the dust of the ages seems to cover some of the oath's wording, it is the term "modernism" that can be misleading. There is nothing mediaeval about the intellectual atmosphere at C.U. One philosophy professor remarked: "After taking the oath, we are liable to end up arguing among ourselves on what *is* modernism. That oath is mainly a formality."

Campus types range from archconservatives and organization men to individualists and liberals who differ on intellectual, administrative and, of late, on architectural matters. Those with conventional tastes speak glowingly of the architecture and the lavish fittings of the National Shrine of the Immaculate Conception, which crowns the campus. Others agree with the professor who described it as a hodgepodge: "If a student in the architecture department turned in such a design as a term project, he would flunk the course." There is also some restlessness among the individualists on campus who chafe under the careful, cautious administration of the University. But the institution's policies are understandable. C.U. is highly visible up there on the summit of Catholic higher education and it has a demanding Board of Trustees composed of United States cardinals and bishops. This close contact is reflected by the fact that Msgr. McDonald follows in the footsteps of eight previous rectors, all of whom eventually became bishops.

Financially, Catholic University is tied to every Catholic parish in the country by the annual collection made in its behalf. As Msgr. McDonald points out in citing the gap between what students pay in tuition and the actual cost of education: "Some schools make up the difference from handsome endowments. The Catholic University of America has no such resources. Its great, life-giving, life-preserving resource is the annual collection taken up for the University once a year throughout the nation. This was and continues to be our salvation."

Educationally, more than 700 Catholic institutions, including colleges, teacher-training schools, nursing schools, secondary schools and seminaries are affiliated with the University in a program of improvement and accreditation. Catholic University acts as a clearinghouse of information and provides evaluation and consultation services. Catholic University's specialized activities include programs in mission studies and pastoral preparation, workshops geared to army chaplains as well as school librarians, adult education with 5,000 students, and a summer session with 4,500 students. It has an Institute of Christian Oriental Research, Child Center, Institute of International Law, Radioisotope Materials Laboratory, Bureau of Social Research, Institute of Ibero-American Studies, even an Arctic Institute and a Herbarium (with 135,000 sheets of mounted specimens collected from Alaska to the Bahamas). When C.U. celebrates its diamond jubilee in 1964, the New Catholic Encyclopedia will be taking shape under the sponsorship of the University and the editorship of Msgr. McDonald. Its fifteen volumes will replace the present fifty-year-old work.

The Commission on American Citizenship, established in 1938 at the suggestion of Pope Pius XI, operates as an arm of the University in offering consulting services to Catholic schools and publishers of textbooks. Its famous Faith and Freedom series is used in more than half of U.S. Catholic elementary schools. The Commission, which assists high schools as well as elementary schools with their curriculum, aims at extending a program of Christian social living in the schools. The Commission also guides over 4,000 civics clubs in Catholic elementary schools.

Expanding along with the rest of American higher education, the University proper completed eleven new buildings in a five-year period ending in 1962, including Keane Physics Research Center, the Nursing Building, Engineering and Architecture Building, residence halls, a social center and an addition to John K. Mullen Memorial Library. The library addition increases capacity to 800,000 volumes, making expansion possible beyond its 600,000 volumes, which are supplemented by 400,000 volumes in the surrounding religious houses of study. Of course, there are also the vast research facilities available in Washington. The library, incidentally, was the first at a Catholic university to pass the half-million mark in number of volumes.

Catholic University's role is dramatized by its 20,000

alumni. They include fifty-seven bishops and forty-two presidents of institutions of higher learning, practically all of them Catholic. There are more than 75 directors and assistant directors of diocesan Catholic charities, 150 professors in 50 major seminaries, hundreds of teachers on all levels of education, and thousands of priests, including almost more than 350 with doctoral degrees in canon law serving in diocesan chanceries or other key posts. Its lay alumni, many of them in leading positions in government, politics, science, the professions and the arts, write Broadway hits and best-sellers (Jean Kerr), lead political parties (Democratic National Chairman John M. Bailey), hold key government positions (Comptroller of the Currency James Saxton).

For the temporary visitor, after living in the newly built Conaty Hall with students who refer to it as the Conaty Hilton, The Catholic University of America is a confrontation with the growing intellectual maturity of American Catholicism. Back in 1889, James Cardinal Gibbons of Baltimore, who received the original letter of approval from Pope Leo XIII for establishing Catholic University, wrote the pontiff about the inauguration of the University, making it clear that from the start this University was thrust into a central position:

On Wednesday, the 13th, in spite of the bad weather, the bishops, priests, and faithful went en masse to Washington for the inauguration of the university. There, as in Baltimore, everything went well. The President of the United States, the vice president, the secretary of state, and several members of the cabinet made it a point to honor this festivity with their presence, and the applause which burst forth when Your health was proposed and which followed the answer of Msgr. Satolli to this toast, as well as that which greeted the President, manifest greatly that the love of the church and the love of the country are indissolubly united in the hearts of the faithful.

While there was disagreement at the time on where to locate the University, it is significant that a generous laywoman carried the day with her preference for Washington, D.C. Miss Mary Gwendoline Caldwell of Newport, Rhode Island, donated $300,000 for establishment of the University in Washington. In retrospect, it is clear that no other city would be appropriate for The Catholic University of America than its suitably symbolic location in the capital of the United States.

UNIVERSITY OF
NOTRE DAME

The Will to Win

WHEN the Rev. Theodore M. Hesburgh, C.S.C., steps into his president's box (C-44) on the 50-yard line at Notre Dame Stadium and joins 59,000 partisans on a Saturday afternoon during *the* season, a glance to the left is reassuring. Looking down on the stadium—probably with condescension—is the tower of the new 13-story Memorial Library, a more accurate symbol of Notre Dame's celebrated will to win than the embarrassing performance of recent football teams. The library epitomizes the Notre Dame formula as summed up by Father Hesburgh in an interview appearing in the 1961 college yearbook: "Football has contributed to Notre Dame and may yet well contribute more. But we are more than football. We are a university, committed to the pursuit of excellence in all its human forms. Let us neglect no one of them: the spiritual, the intellectual, the moral, the cultural, the physical. This is not just a list; it is a hierarchy." And always the aim is to be on top: Notre Dame officials have even figured out that the new $8-million library has more floor area than that of any other university library in the world.

Displacing what was once a floodlit football practice field, the library faces the stadium with a new Computer Center running interference on the left and a new Radiation Laboratory on the right. This is the Notre Dame of today and tomorrow. The theme of the famous "Victory March" is still appropriate ("What though the odds be great or small? Old Notre Dame will win over all"), but the big game is being played every day in libraries, laboratories and classrooms. The campus elite are Woodrow Wilson, Danforth, National Science and Fulbright fellows, though there is plenty of room for an All-American as long as he maintains a 2.0 average (1.0 is passing). In his office, after giving a pep talk to campus drumbeaters for the Peace Corps, Father Hesburgh adds his refrain to the "Victory March": "Football brought out the will to win and we want to have the same in the academic, the will to measure ourselves against the best anywhere."

As an institution, Notre Dame invariably has thrived under a strong leader, playing the game with a maximum of publicity, an impressive record and incomparable self-assurance. With everyone at Notre Dame cheering for academic excellence, the school appears to be succeeding, even though the odds are great against a self-sustaining institution on the northern limits of Indiana, and the cost in the millions. *Time* magazine, impressed by the Notre Dame image, told the story of Catholic higher education in the 1960's by putting Father Hesburgh on the cover and devoting most of its report to Notre Dame.

As Notre Dame entered the 1960's, Father Hesburgh publicly described the University with the following set of superlatives in relation to other Catholic universities: "It has the oldest Law School, one of the few Engineering and Architectural Schools, the only Mediaeval Institute, and is by far the most advanced American Catholic university in the field of science and research. It has, again by far, the finest physical plant of this group, and an endowment greater than any of the others. Its alumni contribute more annually and in vastly larger numbers. Its graduates have won more Woodrow Wilson Fellowships, Danforth Fellowships, Marshall Fellowships and Rhodes Scholarships than all of the other Catholic universities combined. It consistently ranks first in the Catholic group as to winners of Fulbright and National Science Fellowships. Its administration also has been called upon continually for Catholic leadership in educational and public affairs."

According to English Professor Richard Sullivan, who has spent about thirty years on the campus and has described his love affair with Notre Dame in a book of reminiscences, "Notre Dame is a place, a sequence in time, and an immediate, living fact all wrapped round with people." It is also 120 years of continuous ambition wrapped in a magnificent campus, a man's world where the discipline until recently resembled life in a French boarding school for boys, a deeply religious place where it is fashionable to look down upon the college courses in theology. Notre Dame is a flamboyant public image, covered with green and purple patches painted on by imaginative sportswriters who once claimed that the students trotted to class playing catch with footballs. It is a school with a notoriously faithful subway alumni whose memory is as long as a gridiron and as fleeting as a Saturday afternoon in October. Admired for its brawn, it is determined to be respected for its brains, both victim and beneficiary of a dazzling football fame that has had more honor off campus than on. Notre Dame has trouble explaining itself.

French in name, Irish in many of its traditions, typically American in its obsession with victory, Notre Dame has many labels, ranging from City of the Blessed Sacrament to a university known for nothing but football (applied in the 1930's by columnist Westbrook Pegler, among others). Referring to its role as a Catholic university in a pluralistic society, Father Hesburgh calls Notre Dame "a bridge as well as a beacon." Referring to the University's $66,000,000 building program, the irreverent campus magazine, *The Scholastic*, in the spring of 1962, headlined an article, "the Oedifice Complex and Notre Dame." Father Charles E. Sheedy, Dean of the College of Arts and Letters, stressed that "Notre Dame is the largest private men's college in the world."

Notre Dame's executive vice president, Father Edmund P. Joyce, who minds the store while his president

dashes off to Vatican City, Washington, D.C., Geneva
or Peru, describes "a completely self-sufficient community." Its 60 major buildings have a replacement value
of $70 million, with another $25 million in buildings
to be added by the end of 1963. On its 1,000 acres, which
include two natural lakes and a golf course, Notre Dame
has its own police and fire departments, its own branch
of the U.S. Post Office, a bus shelter, a hotel, a central
laundry and steam plant, and its own commercial radio
and television stations. It draws its own water from wells,
generates its own electric power, prints books, cleans
and mends clothes, repairs shoes, cuts hair. Some 1,850
employees keep this community functioning, including
the operator of the movie projector for the free Saturday matinee and evening movies. Notre Dame has everything, except girls; a fellow has to go off campus for a
date.

Academically, Notre Dame is dominated by its undergraduate students who outnumber both law and graduate students by five-and-a-half to one. The undergraduates attend one of four colleges: Arts and Letters, Science,
Engineering, or Business Administration. During the
1961–1962 academic year, there were 5,658 college students and 156 law students, 98 percent of them Catholic,
the overwhelming majority products of Catholic high
schools, three-quarters of them living on campus. The
geographical spread of the student body, reflecting the
length and breadth of the Notre Dame image, is particularly unusual for Catholic schools, which tend to be
regional. States contributing the most students to Notre
Dame were Indiana (945 students), New York (899),

Illinois (892), Ohio (506), Pennsylvania (460), Michigan (372), New Jersey (339), Massachusetts (205), California (199). The states next in line carry through the coast-to-coast mixture at Notre Dame: Wisconsin, Missouri, Connecticut, Minnesota, Texas, Iowa, Kentucky, Maryland, Florida, Kansas, Louisiana, Colorado.

Although the Law and Graduate Schools also draw students nationally, they are small enterprises. The Law School, which was established in 1869, and regards itself as the country's leading small law school, intends to keep enrollment under 300 in any future expansion. It draws 40 percent of its students from Notre Dame College. The Graduate School, focus of the University's ambitions, has only 25 departments, at least one glaring omission (no psychology department), some notable pioneering, some outstanding departments. But it only has 543 male day students. Its total enrollment of 795 is augmented by 78 sisters attending days as well as 132 men and 42 laywomen attending evening classes.

By any standard, Notre Dame is a quality college, providing a first-rate education to a devoted and devout student body, more national in origin than Harvard and comparing favorably with the latter in the number of exceptional students. It is not a football factory (and never was); neither is it a great university (though eventually it may become one). More than any Catholic college, Notre Dame has invited comparisons at the summit and second-best is a subversive notion from Father Hesburgh's office to the stadium locker room. In his interview in the 1961 college yearbook, Father Hesburgh sounded like a coach at the half-time of the season's big game: "Let me say one last thing that may or may not be appreciated. Personally, I desire one quality for Notre Dame: *dedicated excellence* in all the broad educational endeavor that goes on here: intellectually, morally, physically. I would rather see Notre Dame die than be educationally mediocre."

Robert M. Hutchins, formerly chancellor of the University of Chicago and one of the century's leading figures in American higher education, has called "the Notre Dame efflorescence one of the most spectacular developments in higher education in the last 25 years." He also turned the compliment into faint praise by adding: "I suspect that Notre Dame has done more than any other institution in this period, possibly because there was more to do."

As personality cults have always flourished at Notre Dame, it is no surprise that Father Hesburgh has become the Knute Rockne of the University's academic success story. As *Time* noted in its February 9, 1962, cover story: "At 35, Hesburgh became Notre Dame's 16th president. What Hesburgh inherited was a university ready for take-off." The record bears this out. For instance, when Father Hesburgh took over in 1952, Notre Dame had only one Danforth Fellowship winner (that year the football team won 7, lost 2, tied 1). In 1953, there were two Woodrow Wilson Fellowship winners (the football team won 9, tied 1); in 1960, 15 Woodrow Wilson fellows, two Danforths, six Fulbrights, one Rhodes (football team won 2, lost 8); and in 1961, 14 Woodrow Wilsons, two Fulbrights, one Danforth (football team won 5, lost 5).

Nothing happens in obscurity at Notre Dame. In October, 1961, *Look* described "a new kind of sixty-minute man" and reported that Father Hesburgh "has given the stiff arm to that unique zealot, the Notre Dame football fan, who is now muttering because the Fighting Irish have fallen from muscular grace." However, at Notre Dame nobody blames Father Hesburgh for the decline of football, though he has certainly stolen its thunder. The Holy Cross Fathers, along with the students, felt that the 1961 team was as strong as any in the past and were hoping for a national championship. The University's top officials point out that the football policy has not changed: football players still get free room, board and tuition. In fact, the number of scholarships has been increased. But while the University gained Father Hesburgh, the football team lost Coach Frank Leahy, the perfectionist whose teams won 87 games, lost only 11 and tied 9. His successor, campus favorite Terry Brennan, never made the mark as a Notre Dame coach and was fired, certainly proof that football is not dead at Notre Dame. The University, which has had to learn to live with the nation's sportswriters, then had to endure coast-to-coast wailing over Brennan's firing at Christmastime. Joe Kuharich, Brennan's successor, has also been disappointing, though campus opinion is divided on his merits as a coach. His contract runs until 1965. Notre Dame still wants to win over all.

During Father Hesburgh's first ten years as president (1952–1962) Notre Dame has made several giant steps forward. It has won twice as many Woodrow Wilson Fellowships as the Catholic college with the second highest number; nationally, it is in the top ten in winning these fellowships for prospective professors, an increasingly popular indicator of academic excellence. The amount of outside sponsored research rose almost tenfold, reaching $3 million awarded for 80 projects during the 1962–1963 academic year. Notre Dame is now conducting the most extensive research on radiation chemistry on any campus this side of the Iron Curtain. The University's budget for academic salaries rose in ten years from $1.5 to $5 million, the total budget from $8 to $22 million. The salaries of full professors have doubled and now average $12,000 a year, and can run as high as $18,000. There are 116 more faculty Ph.D.'s than ten years ago; the number of faculty research projects and publications has quadrupled. Department heads have a standing order: Keep a file of the best available men in your field; hire them when possible.

Along with the rest of the nation's colleges, Notre Dame has been consistently raising its admission requirements, but at a more rapid rate. Because of its prestige in the Catholic field, Notre Dame has a pick of outstanding Catholic high school graduates. Three times as many winners of National Merit Scholarships go to Notre Dame as go to the next most popular Catholic college. Between 1954 and 1961, Notre Dame raised the average score of its freshmen by 76 points on verbal ability in the College Board tests, by 77 points in math. The students in Arts and Letters and Science have the strongest academic profiles; 89 percent of the 1962 freshmen were in the upper third of their high school classes, 80 percent of the science freshmen were in the upper fifth. In recent

years, Arts and Letters has displaced Business Administration as the largest undergraduate college, reflecting
a shift from a vocational to an academic orientation on
the part of students.

Notre Dame's crucial recognition was achieved when
it became one of five universities selected by the Ford
Foundation for its "Special Program in Education." The
five were chosen, the Ford Foundation announced, "on
the basis of their geographical location, excellence of
leadership, strength of constituency, strategic importance to other universities of the same type and in the
same region, a tradition of scholarship or clear evidence
of a desire and ability to achieve it, and plans to move
forward toward greater scholarly accomplishment." The
Ford Foundation placed $6 million in reserve for Notre
Dame between July 1, 1960, and June 30, 1963; for every
two dollars Notre Dame collected, Ford would send
one, meaning if Notre Dame collected $12 million over
those three years, it would be $18 million richer. The
money was promptly earmarked: $8 million for the new
library, $2 million for student aid, $4 million for graduate
residence halls, $3.5 million for a faculty fund, one-half
million for the administrative fund. Notre Dame, incidentally, decided to raise $18 million instead of only $12
million in that period.

Possibly no other college in the country—Catholic or
secular—inspires such passionate devotion as Notre
Dame. Its famous spirit is genuine; the label, Notre Dame
man, is worn with pride and, even if some of the wearers
are indifferent, they discover it is a very useful label,
whether they are trying to impress a date or a future

employer. The story is told of G. K. Chesterton's appearance at the dedication of Notre Dame stadium while he was on campus for a series of lectures in the fall of 1930. As the celebrated author mounted the platform, the audience of 20,000 shouted a cheer that still fills the stadium on football Saturdays: "He's a man! Who's a man? He's a Notre Dame man!" Chesterton, unaware that he was receiving the finest conceivable compliment, turned nervously to a companion and remarked, "My, they're angry!" When he was told, "Angry? Golly, man, they're cheering you!" he broke into a fit of laughter. (It is not clear whether he laughed at the local custom or his own confusion.)

Of course, part of the explanation for the Notre Dame spirit lies in the fact that young men congregate on its self-contained campus in a tightly knit community and live out four impressionable and crucial years. In explaining his attachment to Notre Dame, Richard Sullivan, who came to the school as an undergraduate, reminisced: "It's like this: you start thinking and you remember that, around twenty, as an undergraduate, you somehow came alive. It might have happened to you in any number of places, but it did in fact happen in one, which you therefore recall with special clarity. People there influenced you once and forever. You were confronted for the first time with ideas, abstractions bigger than life; with principles which had a power to govern and control; with philosophy, a tremendous, violent, electric experience for a mind previously occupied only with sensation."

For the average freshman, becoming a Notre Dame man is an overwhelming, unforgettable experience. He

reaches out quickly for the label; according to salesgirls
at the campus bookstore, the average freshman invariably buys a lamp, a desk blotter and a windbreaker, all
displaying the N.D. imprint. Before he can turn around,
the new freshman is caught up in Saturday football
games when thousands of fans descend upon the
campus, creating an autumnal Mardi Gras. Rarely can
a young man, fresh out of high school, ignore the spirit
in the air when the leaves begin to fall and the "Victory
March" echoes through the stadium.

Before the first year is over, the N.D. freshman has
been dazzled, driven, convinced, stimulated, over-
whelmed, and absorbed into the Notre Dame community.
He seldom resists and in fact he becomes so attached that
Notre Dame becomes the only school for him. It is common to hear students talk about classmates who were
thrown out of Notre Dame or suspended, but still long to
return. In the course of one coke at the "Huddle," a
campus snack shop, the boys at my table told about one
classmate who was suspended for three semesters. Instead of transferring elsewhere, he is waiting to return
to Notre Dame. Another friend, who was thrown out
after only three semesters, developed such a strong attachment that he flew up from Florida for a football
game and visited his old friends. One social science professor reported that he advises several students a year
interested in psychology to transfer elsewhere, since
Notre Dame doesn't offer psychology and the students
will lose a year in graduate school making up undergraduate courses. None ever leaves Notre Dame.

Father Thomas T. McAvoy, who has spent a lifetime at Notre Dame and is beloved as a personality and respected as a historian, describes three major elements in the Notre Dame spirit: the frequent Holy Communion, the competitive spirit brought out by football successes, and the family spirit. Elaborating on the latter, another Notre Dame old-timer, Alumni Director James Armstrong, points out: "The students have a total interest in the total University. They are not split into small groups but are completely mingled in the student body. The University has retained a fundamental physical identity as well as a nucleus of religious and lay faculty. No matter how old the alumnus returning for a visit, he usually finds some old professor or priest whom he used to know still on campus. Here at Notre Dame there is a combination of the changing and the unchanging."

Not even a disciplinary system that has been described as second only to West Point or Annapolis has dampened enthusiasm for Notre Dame. Only after a private and well documented indictment was drawn up by the students, who showed that the disciplinary rules were Jansenistic as well as unrealistic, were the rules modified in the fall of 1961. Somehow, the students put up for years with a system that required the pulling of a master switch turning off all lights for the freshmen at 11 P.M. and for the rest of the college at midnight. Students were also forced—in effect—to attend Mass three mornings a week. To quote from page 24 of the 1960–1961 Student Manual: "Every campus student must make morning check personally and fully dressed three times a week at the time and place designated by the Rector [invariably at the Chapel door]. Although morning check does not require the student to attend any service in the hall chapel, such as Mass or morning prayer, it is an encouragement for him to do so."

No more apt historical footnote to Notre Dame discipline can be found than in the October, 1890, remark of the Rev. Thomas E. Walsh, who was Notre Dame's strong hand at the helm from 1881 to 1893. After expelling a group of students who went off campus without permission and proceeded to spend a very late evening drinking, Father Walsh said: "It is better to have a small attendance at the University with good discipline than a large attendance without it. The rules will be preserved at any cost."

How did Notre Dame maintain for so many decades its rules with a handful of priests managing thousands of young men full of animal spirits and occasionally with other spirits? There are many answers, some differing with the individual, but all throwing light on the Notre Dame personality. First, it is certainly true that evasion was a highly developed art; it is not so clear how widespread the evasion. You hear from some students that everyone has a bottle in his room, from others that they don't know anyone with a bottle in his room. Other students report that there are always enough open windows so a student can slip in unnoticed late at night, that football players manage to make end runs around the rules. As to the lights-out rule, the electrical engineering students used to provide special rewiring services. For $2, you could get wired into the alternate electrical system that had to operate all the time to light up the halls and the washrooms. For $5, the deluxe job would turn off the lights as soon as the rector turned your doorknob. Depending on the individual student, the unwritten rule may have been: "Don't get caught."

Certainly, this all-male community needed escape valves and still does, though the compulsory blackout and early morning chapel check were discontinued in the fall of 1961. Athletics is a major outlet whose dimensions extend far beyond the autumnal football ecstasy, even beyond the other intercollegiate sports, particularly basketball. Intramural sports and informal games flourish on campus; at times the campus resembles a giant boys' camp with students playing catch, having half-court basketball games, throwing the plastic Frisbie disc back and forth. (The latter invites the special scorn of campus intellectuals.) One graduate student from Brooklyn said he was appalled by the number of students hobbling around on crutches during football season, not from intercollegiate games but from intramural rough tackle. Here, he was undoubtedly succumbing to the general tendency to exaggerate anything connected with Notre Dame. There are actually very few major injuries in intramural football, though there are plenty of minor ones, and, moreover, intramural football is on the wane.

Occasionally, the students become rebellious enough to assert themselves but not so much as to constitute a revolution. There was the cherished time in the 1950's when they broke all the glasses in the dining hall because their milk ration was being cut back by replacing 8-ounce glasses with 6-ounce ones. Or the time hundreds of spoiled steaks were stacked in front of the dining

room manager's door. Or the Saturday evening in the
spring of 1962 when a thousand students engaged in a
battle of water hoses. At one dormitory, wastebaskets
were added to the barrage. The crowd moved onto the
bus shelter where they rocked incoming buses; one bus
filled with girls arriving for a mixer turned right around
and went home. No police were needed, the dean of
students waved his hands and the crowd calmed down.

On campus, Notre Dame students are probably the
worst-dressed college boys in the nation. At the evening meals when they are supposed to wear a jacket and
tie, they achieve highly imaginative feats of conformity
to the letter of the law and total rejection of its spirit.
Visible on the dining room line is the most bizarre assort-
ment of dress this side of Skid Row. Here are samples:
students with four-in-hands draped around their necks
like scarves, a clip-on tie dangling precariously from
one collar, ties worn over shirt collars, a bow tie clipped
to a white T-shirt, a red four-in-hand worn over a white
T-shirt and under a solid red jacket. Then there was a
memorable jacket made of strips of faded red, white
and blue cloth; sewed onto the back was a pink triangle
with a white star in the middle. The faculty reports that
a Notre Dame man arrives as a freshman with a fine
collegiate wardrobe and his dress becomes progressively
more chaotic the longer he is at Notre Dame. The
students say that a Notre Dame man is a fashion plate
when going out, but the unwritten student law on campus is to dress informally. It is the uniform of belonging
and it probably represents passive resistance to the mani-
fold rules and regulations that surround life at Notre

Dame. Probably the best way to improve dress at Notre Dame is to announce that students don't have to wear jackets and ties to dinner. It would also deprive the students of an outlet, and an opportunity to express their individuality.

The Holy Cross Fathers are particularly proud of the "spectacular Catholicism" practiced by Notre Dame students, though a minority view was expressed by a leading social scientist on campus. He observed that "religion is fully automated at Notre Dame. The student presses a button in the church or at the Chaplain's office and a priest pops up to hear his confession. He falls out of bed in the morning and into Mass at the Chapel in his residence hall. It is totally unrealistic and unlike what the student faces after college." Every one of the 17 residence halls has a Chapel where three or four Masses are celebrated every morning and Masses are celebrated all morning long at the student church.

Despite abolition of the morning check and its indirect pressure toward attendance at Mass, the number of students attending Mass and receiving Communion remains breathtaking. The student chaplain estimates that one-third of the students go to Mass and Communion every day, one-half go at least every other day. A Holy Cross Brother works full time making 25,000 Communion hosts a week plus another 1,500 large hosts. A drop-off in Mass and Communion is reflected, however, in the fewer hosts he is making; before relaxation of the rules he was making 30,000 hosts a week. The chaplain also reported a drop-off, while agreeing with the majority view that Notre Dame's "spiritual observ-

ance is more towards the spectacular than the automatic." However, he finds the number of religious vocations disappointing; only 11 students joined the Holy
Cross Order in 1961, nine in 1960, 12 in 1959. The proba-
ble reason is that by the time students arrive at Notre
Dame, they are career-oriented; the decision to enter the
religious life is typically made during or immediately
after high school.

Another noteworthy side of the religious activity at
Notre Dame is the string of novenas, running from one
end of the school year to the next. The students pray for
their mothers, for success in examinations, on behalf of
the young lady they are taking to the prom; on the morning of football games they go to Mass and Communion to
pray that "no one will be injured." It is no secret that
this is Notre Dame's disguise for a Victory Prayer.

Football, a nostalgia for college, a feeling of belonging, a sense of fulfillment—Notre Dame seems to have
drawn all of them together in its religious life. Its total
religious framework was described from the vantage
point of an outsider for the alumni magazine. Rabbi Albert L. Plotkin of Phoenix, Arizona, who as a native of
South Bend attended Notre Dame, wrote that "the first
thing for which I had great admiration for Notre Dame
was the fact that it infused within its students a feeling
that religion must become part and parcel of one's entire being." The aura of religion produces individual
flashes of drama for Notre Dame men; in the case of
Dr. Tom Dooley, who captured the imagination of
America, it produced one of the most dramatic testimonials in the history of Notre Dame. It came in a per-

sonal letter to Father Hesburgh, though its text is now on public display at the University's Grotto of Our Lady of Lourdes, a replica of the shrine at Lourdes. The date was December 2, 1960, the place Hong Kong, the contents so memorable that it would be unfair to the meaning of Notre Dame and the personal dimensions of one man's faith not to quote it in full:

Dear Father Hesburgh,

They've got me down. Flat on the back . . . with plaster, sand bags and hot water bottles. It took the last three instruments to do it however. I've contrived a way of pumping the bed up a bit so that, with a long reach, I can get to my typewriter . . . my mind . . . my brain . . . my fingers.

Two things prompt this note to you, sir. The first is that whenever my cancer acts up . . . and it is certainly "acting up" now, I turn inward a bit. Less do I think of my hospitals around the world, or of 94 doctors, fund raising and the like. More do I think of one divine Doctor, and my own personal fund of grace. Is it enough?

It has become pretty definite that the cancer has spread to the lumbar vertebrae, accounting for all the back problems over the last two months. I have monstrous phantoms . . . as all men do. But I try to exorcise them with all the fury of the Middle Ages. And inside and outside the wind blows.

But when the time comes, like now, then the storm around me does not matter. The winds within me do not matter. Nothing human or earthly can touch me. A wilder storm of peace gathers in my heart. What seems unpossessable, I can possess. What seems unfathomable, I fathom. What is unutterable, I can utter. Because I can pray. I can communicate. How do people endure anything on earth if they cannot have God?

I realize the external symbols that surround one when he prays are not important. The stark wooden cross on an altar of boxes in Haiphong with a tortured priest . . . the magnificence of the Sacred Heart Bernini altar . . . they are essentially the same. Both are symbols. It is the Something else there that counts.

But just now . . . and just so many times, how I long for the Grotto. Away from the Grotto Dooley just prays. But at the Grotto, especially now when there must be snow everywhere and the lake is ice glass and that triangular fountain on the left is frozen solid and all the priests are bundled in their too-large too-long old black coats and the students wear snow boots . . . If I could go to the Grotto now, then I think I could sing inside. I could be full of faith and poetry and loveliness and know more beauty, tenderness and compassion. This is soggy sentimentalism, I know. Cold prayers from a hospital bed are just as pleasing to God as more youthful prayers from a Grotto on the lid of night.

But like telling a mother in labor, "It's okay, millions have endured the labor pains and survived happy . . . you will too." It's consoling . . . but doesn't lessen the pain. Accordingly, knowing prayers from here are just as good as from the Grotto doesn't lessen my gnawing, yearning passion to be there.

I don't mean to ramble. Yes, I do.

The second reason I write to you just now is that I have in front of me the Notre Dame *Alumnus* of September, 1960. And herein is a story. This is a Chinese hospital run by a Chinese division of the Sisters of Charity (I think). Though my doctors are British the hospital is as Chinese as Shark's Fin Soup. Every orderly, corpsman, nurse and nun knows of my work in Asia, and each has taken it upon himself to personally "give" to the man they feel has given to their Asia. As a consequence I'm a bit smothered in tender, loving care.

With a triumphant smile this morning one of the nuns

brought me some American magazines (which are limp
with age and which I must hold horizontal above my head
to read . . .). An old *National Geographic,* two older *Times,*
and that unfortunate edition *Life* . . . and with these, a
copy of the Notre Dame *Alumnus.* How did it ever get
here?

So, Father Hesburgh, Notre Dame is twice on my mind
. . . and always in my heart. That Grotto is the rock to
which my life is anchored. Do the students ever appreciate
what they have, while they have it? I know I never did.
Spent most of my time being angry at the clergy at school
. . . 10 P.M. bed check, absurd for a 19-year-old veteran,
etc., etc., etc. Won't take any more of your time, did just
want to communicate for a moment, and again offer my
thanks to my beloved Notre Dame. Though I lack a certain
buoyancy in my bones just now, I lack none in my spirit.
I must return to the states very soon, and I hope to sneak
into that Grotto . . . before the snow has melted.

My best wishes to the students, regards to the faculty,
and respects to you.

Very sincerely,
Tom Dooley

While religion has the honored place on the Notre
Dame campus, the school's religious program is not above
student criticism. In fact, the students complain openly
about the sermons in church, the daily religious bulletins
and, most of all, about the quality of the required theology courses. Editorialized *The Scholastic,* sounding
board for all campus complainers: "The main troubles
with most of the sermons at Sacred Heart [the University church] have been that they have tended toward
simplistic moral admonitions proceeding from ridicu-
lously elaborate metaphorical constructs; have tried to

say too much, with a pretense of arriving at a truth with theoretical rigor; or have used the Gospel as a 'jumping-off point' for a sermon unrelated to the message of the day." Some campus intellectuals complain that the daily religious bulletin is addressed to the twelve-year-old mind, a far cry from its popularity in the days when Father John Francis O'Hara (later Notre Dame president and eventually Cardinal O'Hara) was Prefect of Religion. With the Bulletin, which was an immediate success when he established it in 1921, Father O'Hara sought to apply "modern principles of advertising to the spiritual life."

Whereas on some Catholic campuses the required theology courses are endured passively by students as advanced classes in catechism and assigned to priests as a teaching sideline, Notre Dame students are demanding better theology courses and there is considerable academic commotion surrounding the theology department. Father Hesburgh, a former head of the department, has shown particular interest in a problem which he stated in a theology textbook, *God and the World of Man*. He directed the textbook at a laity "who today have become increasingly mindful of their need for a deeper knowledge of the truths of Theology in order to participate more intelligently in the great lay movements of liturgical revival and Catholic Action that characterize our age." Progress is such at Notre Dame that Father Hesburgh's book is already regarded as outmoded.

When *Time* pointed out that "all students and most faculty members" regard theology as the worst department on campus, the present head of the department responded with an essay on "Theological Dynamism at Notre Dame" for the alumni magazine. It is noteworthy that he did not deny or affirm the charge; he prudently pointed out that the department is constantly improving. He noted that the theology department had one Ph.D. in 1946; today 16 out of its 27 members have doctorates or the equivalent. He cited the Summer Graduate Program in Theology with 200 students, and the first of six yearly institutes for religious superiors (with 1,000 applications for the summer of 1962). He could also have added that the Notre Dame theology textbooks are best-sellers in their field. The turning point for theology teaching at Notre Dame came about in 1946 with a policy decision to have theologians, not the nearest and most available priest, teach theology. In the years since that decision, Notre Dame has been a leading modernizer in the teaching of theology, but it still has a way to go to satisfy student and faculty critics.

On the undergraduate level, English and history are regarded as leading departments at Notre Dame, with mathematics and the social sciences improving rapidly. Notre Dame is strong in all engineering departments; its electrical engineers have been particularly successful in winning National Science Foundation Fellowships, comparing favorably with the prestige engineering universities.

While it is difficult to compare student bodies, the general opinion at Notre Dame is that its top students compare with any in the country and get as sound a preparation as they could get anywhere. Under the supervision of a Committee on Academic Progress, exceptional students are given free rein to move as quickly as they feel able, selecting courses across the board. Possibly, Notre Dame does not do as well with middle and lower-ranking students, but the administration would disagree strongly with this judgment. A professor, who taught at Yale, insisted that the top students were on a par in both places, the middle group more interested in their studies at Notre Dame, the lower group at Notre Dame inferior.

As a student body, Notre Dame men are unusually homogeneous. They tend to come from upper-middle-class families, their fathers are college graduates who are business or professional men. About a fourth of the students help pay their way with part-time jobs, scholarships and loans. Since the students must board, except for a few who come from the surrounding area, a student's family must be able to afford $2,500 in basic costs for each year away at college. There are few Negroes at Notre Dame (they are welcome, but few apply); there are few representatives of America's newer minority groups. Catholic, upper-middle-class, with a tendency to be politically conservative, Notre Dame is far from the seething intellectual and social influences of the big cities that affect other large Catholic universities. Notre Dame may not be a Catholic ghetto, but neither is it a micro-cosm of a pluralistic society.

The graduate student body has only slightly more variety than the undergraduate. Of those graduate students who indicated their religion, 85.5 percent were Catholic; there were 54 Protestants, six Jews. Only 2 percent of all students came from abroad; there were nine Negroes, 16 of Asiatic origin in the graduate school. Besides 27 Canadians, the only foreign countries with more than ten students at Notre Dame were India (15) and Colombia (11). There were only four students from Africa in the entire 1961–1962 student body.

A strong indictment of the Notre Dame atmosphere was drawn up by one of its recent favored sons, Jerry Brady of the class of 1958. A former president of the student body and later personal secretary to Father Hesburgh on a tour of Africa and Europe, Brady looked back in indignation at what he called "parochial activism" and "general stupefaction in public life at Notre Dame." During his third year at the Law School of the University of California at Berkeley, Brady wrote in the February 23, 1962, issue of *The Scholastic:* "Believe me, when I came to the University of California in 1959 I tried to maintain my prejudices. But I couldn't. I had to admit that my fellow students were doing a service to their University, which we Catholics had not done for ours, by plunging it into debate on important matters." (The 1962 senior class at Notre Dame voted comedian Bob Hope its annual Patriotism Award for entertaining American servicemen.)

Notre Dame is self-centered partly because it is not likely to be stimulated by the city of South Bend, its sluggish, industrial neighbor struggling to maintain employment levels. The students are not indifferent, but they tend to avoid making connections between passing issues and universal truths. They are engrossed with Notre Dame, a cohesive spiritual, intellectual, athletic and fraternal community that is not easily intruded upon from the outside. Yet a student body of 6,000 can't be judged with one generalization. For instance, judging from bookstore paperback favorites, they read Albert Camus and Dr. Tom Dooley, Graham Greene and John O'Hara, Salinger and Churchill. A clue to the conservatism of the campus is the popularity of books by William Buckley and by Senator Barry Goldwater. Goldwater had an enthusiastic audience in his spring, 1962, campus appearance, but then so did a faculty discussion on Albert Camus.

Notre Dame's location has affected its personality in a way that is often not taken into account. No large metropolis or major university overshadows the school. Out there in Indiana, neither big city cynicism nor odious comparison dampens what often seems like naïve optimism. It has always seemed at Notre Dame that anything is possible, given a strong faith, hard work and determination. Father Hesburgh's dreams of excellence ring true historically in the Notre Dame story.

Notre Dame has always had a "golden dome mentality." Its founder, Father Edward F. Sorin, insisted on what was an extravagant landmark for a fledgling college—a gold-covered dome and statue of Notre Dame (Our Lady). Campus historians report that Notre Dame's founder left in a huff when his congregation refused to let him have his flamboyant golden dome and statue. He retired to nearby St. Mary's (which became in 1855 the nation's first degree-granting Catholic women's college) until he had his way. The dome and statue have since become the Notre Dame trademark. Notre Dame men claim that on coast-to-coast plane flights the only landmark pointed out by airline pilots is the golden dome. With loving care and at a cost of $50,000, a new coat of gold leaf was applied in the summer of 1961.

Father Sorin founded the college in 1842, meeting what seemed an impossible condition of establishing both a college and novitiate within two years. He obtained the assistance of a Methodist state senator in getting an Indiana charter on January 15, 1844, for "a body corporate and politic, by the name and style of the 'University of Notre Dame du Lac.'" Father Sorin saw his college burn down thirty-five years after its birth, but, always indomitable, he helped rebuild it with his own hands in four months flat.

Father Sorin was interested in good Catholics, not Catholic scholars. In an officially sponsored history of Notre Dame, Father Arthur J. Hope notes that Father Sorin "countenanced no moves that might make of Notre Dame a real university." Fortunately, in December, 1867, a 16-year-old farm boy arrived at Notre Dame with the required "1 table knife, 1 fork, 1 teaspoon, and 1 tablespoon" and the aptitude for scientific scholarship. He became Father John A. Zahm, Notre Dame's only noteworthy scholar of the nineteenth century and eventually University Vice President. At his death in 1921, Notre Dame was emerging as a nationally known university.

Speaking at the golden jubilee of Father Sorin in 1888, Father Zahm spoke in accents recognizable to the Notre Dame of today. He dressed Notre Dame's ambition in academic robes, foreshadowing the present leap forward: "I love to see in our Notre Dame of today the promise

of the potency of a Padua or a Bologna, a Bonn or a
Heidelberg, an Oxford or a Cambridge, a Salamanca or
a Valladolid. It may be this view will be regarded as one
proceeding from my own enthusiasm, but it matters not.
I consider it a compliment to be called an enthusiast."

The two world wars of this century were milestones
in the expansion of Notre Dame. In 1905, it was a small
Midwestern college with 210 students; until 1920, Catholic boys were able to study on its campus from kinder-
garten through graduate school. After World War I,
enrollment passed 2,000. Meanwhile, in 1913, a Nor-
wegian-American Protestant named Knute Rockne and
a little-remembered quarterback named Gus Dorais per-
formed the greatest single miracle in the history of Catholic higher education before a disbelieving crowd at West
Point. The forward passes that went from Dorais to
left end Rockne not only surprised, humiliated and defeated Army, 35 to 13, they transformed a backwoods
Indiana college into a household word. This by no means
explains Notre Dame's success, but it does provide a
dramatic landmark.

The role of football was important to American Catholicism as well as to Notre Dame. It meant that underdog
immigrant groups, for whom life was difficult and vic-
tories few, could cheer a Catholic team to victory. It also
introduced American Catholics to the notion that universities were not godless places of learning; Notre Dame
both played and prayed hard. Said Rockne to a reporter
asking about his success as a coach and the kind of as-
sistants he had: "That fellow over there is my first assistant." The reporter asked who he was. "Father John

O'Hara, the Prefect of Religion. He keeps these fellows fit." Father McAvoy, now the University archivist, recalls that Father O'Hara and Rockne were the two dominant figures at Notre Dame in their overlapping careers. Rockne was coach from 1918 until 1931 when he was killed in a plane crash (holding a rosary—he had been converted to Catholicism). Father O'Hara was Prefect of Religion from 1918 until 1934 when he became president. During those years, Father McAvoy reports, Notre Dame felt it could afford to lose Rockne, but not Father O'Hara, "the greatest single moral influence on campus during the 1920's and early 1930's."

Undoubtedly, football paid off and still does. The current football team pays for itself and the entire athletic program at Notre Dame and still nets about $250,000, which is used for academic expenses. Moreover, football has attracted attention and the helping hand of rich donors. While these donors give for laudable motives, it often happens that they are also rabid football fans. The Associate Board of Lay Trustees, which helps invest university funds, has a much larger turnout for its fall meeting during football season than for its spring meeting. While football rallies supporters around Notre Dame, the consensus among campus old-timers is that it was always more important off campus than on.

As its public image is transformed from the athletic to the academic, Notre Dame intends to stabilize its total enrollment which soared to 5,000 after World War II. The school doesn't plan to participate in the student boom of the 1960's, which means its undergraduate enrollment will become increasingly selective. About one in four applicants is being accepted; the figure could reach one in ten as the resident undergraduate student body remains around 5,500. The graduate school has a goal of 1,000 students, attending full-time and working toward doctorates. Under a policy for a "great university" outlined by Father Hesburgh, Notre Dame will have a full-time faculty and student body, an uncluttered curriculum, extensive facilities, a cosmopolitan faculty and student body, and an environment over which it continues to have complete control. The policy is clearly directed at the situation in which Notre Dame finds itself, though its present student body is certainly not cosmopolitan. Urban universities, with many part-time faculty members and commuting students who also must work, would not define the ideal situation in exactly the same way.

Since the publicized emphasis on excellence invites comparisons, Notre Dame facts, fictions, dreams and realities, and the odds facing them, must be pointed out. Some leading professors on campus find any notion that Notre Dame will stand comparison with Harvard in the near future "naïve." One of the University's leading professors, renowned as teacher, scholar and author, calls the following a reasonable goal: to make Notre Dame one of the top forty United States universities in the next 20 years. Another questioned whether Catholic schools should be in graduate education at all.

Notre Dame has two major handicaps on the graduate level. Its research facilities—with notable exceptions— are inadequate, and it has not attracted enough outstanding graduate students, who, in the current sellers' market, must be recruited much as are football players. They must be offered scholarships and the opportunity to join a winning team. Notre Dame does not have enough scholarships and its graduate departments are not uniformly outstanding. While large urban universities can make up for research deficiencies by drawing on the resources of the city where they are located, Notre Dame has only South Bend. Chicago, 90 miles away, is too far for sustained research work. While it leads Catholic universities in number of library volumes, Notre Dame ranked only 58th nationally in 1961.

The best Catholic college graduates tend to select non-Catholic graduate schools where the Ph.D.'s usually have more prestige and the scholarships are more generous. Ironically, even Catholic colleges and universities like to hire men with secular Ph.D.'s in order to strengthen their departments. In recent years, Notre Dame itself has hired young alumni for its faculty after they earned Ivy League graduate degrees. Notre Dame does not grant sabbaticals to its professors so they can take a year off to carry on full-time research, thereby building reputations for themselves and their academic departments. Aware of this problem, Father Chester A. Soleta, the academic vice president, notes that faculty members can take leaves of absence if they obtain grants and the university will make supplementary payments. Father Soleta says that sabbaticals are on the horizon, but until they materialize, the school suffers from an academic anachronism.

Administratively, Notre Dame has a first-rate team from President Hesburgh through the executive, business, academic and athletic branches. The visitor is im-

pressed by the clear separation of powers under the one
strong hand of Father Hesburgh. The school's administrators speak authoritatively and impressively of their
domains, each certain of his boundaries. Notre Dame still
is dominated by the nineteenth century authoritarian
view of an educational institution with ultimate authority
clearly vested in the man at the top, though it has become more pragmatic and practical in day-to-day operations. The lay faculty can only advise and influence; it
has no real power. No layman has a high administrative
title. Notre Dame's 90 priests are surrounded by a faculty
of 400 laymen and, excluding theology and philosophy,
a priest in the classroom is the exception. The Congregation of the Holy Cross rules and the laymen teach. As
one lay professor remarked, "The lay faculty learns to
live with it." Said another layman of his experience on
the Academic Council of the University: "We had influence, but no power." This lay-religious dichotomy is not
necessarily an insoluble problem, but it is an unresolved
part of the evolution toward tomorrow's Notre Dame.

While some students and faculty members are critical
of their "absentee" president, Father Hesburgh regards
his multiple outside activities as "vital" to the role of the
University. "Everything I do on the outside has reper-
cussions on campus," he remarks. By presidential appointment Father Hesburgh is a member of the U.S. Commission on Civil Rights and the National Science Board; by
papal appointment he is permanent Vatican City representative to the International Atomic Energy Agency.
He has been president of the Association of American
Colleges. He is a director of the Woodrow Wilson Na-

tional Fellowship Corporation, the Nutrition Foundation, the Freedoms Foundation and Educational Service, Inc., of Massachusetts Institute of Technology. He is a member of the Special Studies Group of the Rockefeller Brothers Fund and the Advisory Council of the Institute of European Studies. These are by no means all his outside involvements.

In June, 1962, Brandeis, Massachusetts Institute of Technology and Indiana University awarded him honorary doctorates, adding their honors to a list that already ranged from Columbia and Princeton to the Catholic University of Santiago, Chile. Columbia University said of him: "Mediocrity and social injustice have long been your chosen adversaries; enlightened understanding, your goal; and your armor, a determination to lift man's spirit to nobler things." Father Hesburgh is very much a man of his time, one of those strategically located individuals who emerge to lead complex modern institutions. He has an instinct for the significant, the flexibility and facility that enable him to fill many roles, the physical endurance and personal toughness to maintain a withering schedule and constant public exposure. If Father Hesburgh didn't exist, Notre Dame would have had to invent him in order to pursue its ambitions.

During the ten-year period, 1958–1967, Notre Dame has set a goal of $66.6 million in financial aid; the allotment of this enormous fund indicates the future outlines of its progress. Eleven million dollars will go toward research, $5 million for student aid, $5 million for administrative purposes, $18 million for buildings, including the new library and two graduate halls. The largest single

amount, $27.5 million, will be used for an endowment
for increased faculty salaries. With Notre Dame's instinct for finding the right man, this will mean further
recruitment of top educators and professors. The Notre
Dame touch is best illustrated by its hiring of Dr. George
N. Shuster, who served as president of New York City's
Hunter College for 20 years. Known as an "educator's
educator" and internationally renowned, Dr. Shuster is
the outstanding Catholic layman in higher education.
With him as assistant to Father Hesburgh, Notre Dame
has the most prominent pair of ambassadors in Catholic
higher education. Hiring him was possibly the wisest
personnel move on any Catholic campus in the postwar
period. On the academic side Notre Dame has hired as
dean of the College of Science Dr. Frederick Rossini, a
celebrated chemist and president of the national scientific
fraternity, Sigma Xi.

The allotments can set in motion the chain attraction
that draws in top professors who attract top graduate
students who in turn create a framework for research
work that attracts other professors. Increased facilities,
along with a major expansion in library facilities, will ac-
celerate the process. Notre Dame has nearly doubled the
number of the library's volumes in the past ten years,
passing the 600,000 mark in June, 1961. Faculty members report that they can, in effect, order any books
they want for the library, which in its new quarters can
hold as many as three million volumes by applying modern library techniques.

The new Computer Center, housing a UNIVAC 1107,
will also have an impact on the entire University, ranging from the complications of class schedules to the com-

plexities of metallurgy and chemical engineering, two
fields in which the graduate school is particularly strong.
The new Radiation Laboratory is being underwritten by
the Atomic Energy Commission in recognition of the
school's research in radiation chemistry. The school's
Lobund Laboratory is nationally famous for its research
on germ-free life. Graduate departments, which are regarded highly, include mathematics, history, English and
philosophy. The Mediaeval Institute is unique. The lag
in the social sciences is being closed by active faculty
recruiting and the growing research output of the present staff.

All this will shorten the odds considerably in Notre
Dame's favor on the graduate level; on the undergraduate
level, it is closer to excellence (though its recent failure
to obtain a Phi Beta Kappa chapter was a setback). The
celebrated Notre Dame mystique is the most difficult to
calculate, but it has been demonstrably successful. The
Laetare Medal is an example. Late in the nineteenth century, a group of Holy Cross priests in a little-known
Catholic college in Indiana were taking the air on the
porch after dinner when the conversation turned to the
Catholic laity and the need to encourage its contribution
to American Catholicism. Though some of the priests
thought there would be a dearth of candidates, it was
decided to honor an outstanding American Catholic layman each year. The Holy Cross Fathers took it for
granted that they should do the honoring from their
small hinterland college. What they created, in their
Notre Dame way, was a barometer of the rise of American Catholicism, culminating in 1961 with the awarding
of the Laetare Medal to a Catholic President. The cita-

tion, read and presented by Father Hesburgh in the
White House, said: "Today (Nov. 12, 1961), deeply
moved, we present to you, Mr. President, the greatest
honor Notre Dame can bestow upon a Catholic layman
in the United States, the Laetare Medal, awarded every
year since 1883 to signalize and encourage the distinguished achievement of individual Catholic citizens in
America."

In June, 1960, Notre Dame had commencement exercises that brought to its platform the President of the
United States (Eisenhower), a Prince of the Church
(Cardinal Montini of Milan) and the President of the
United Nations General Assembly (Dr. Víctor Andrés
Belaúnde). At a dramatic moment in the proceedings,
Dr. Tom Dooley, whom everyone knew was gravely
ill, received an honorary degree along with this distinguished company. President Eisenhower stopped the
ceremony to get up personally to congratulate this devoted Notre Dame man. Another Notre Dame man, Dr.
George Shuster, was given the Laetare Medal at the
ceremonies.

At this summit graduation, bringing together figures
at the pinnacle of Church, government, and international diplomacy, along with distinguished sons of Notre
Dame, the mystique received its full dramatization.
This unabashed assignment to itself of a place at the
summit distinguishes Notre Dame most of all; a football
pass on the playing fields of West Point is only a footnote
to a grand soaring mystique of victory that can make
Notre Dame a favorite in its pursuit of excellence.

ST. LOUIS UNIVERSITY

"Ratio Studiorum" on the Mississippi

ST. LOUIS UNIVER-
SITY, the first university west of the Mississippi, has
grown up with its city, sharing growing pains, suffering
from urban sprawl, and, now, participating in its face-
lifting. The University traces its history to 1818, one year
after a dashing river pilot brought the first steamer to the
St. Louis wharf, beginning the city's golden days of expansion in trade and population. During its first fifty
years, after enduring, along with St. Louis, the Know-
Nothing movement, pestilence and the Civil War, the
University bought property in 1867 at a mud crossroads
called Grand and Lindell. This has been its permanent
location in the heart of the city ever since.

Ninety-five years later, after living beside some of the city's worst slums and being forced to scatter its rapidly expanding academic operations, the University took over a 22-acre lot that had been cleared of slums by the city. One block away from the original mud crossroads, the vacant lot looked equally unpromising. Within two hours after full legal possession was completed—on the Ides of March, 1962—St. Louis broke ground for a three-story physics building, a milestone in a monumental effort to consolidate its operations. St. Louis University was anxious, after so many years, to pull itself together.

The past, present and part of the University's future are visible on a walk east along West Pine Boulevard toward Grand and the vacant lot. Marquette Hall, a shiny new dormitory built for women as Marguerite Hall and temporarily housing male freshmen, casts its shadow upon a genteel-looking mansion that has been converted, appropriately, into the School of Social Service. Following in confusion are Notre Dame Hall for student nuns, the offices of Typographical Union No. 8, St. Francis Xavier Elementary and High schools, and the St. Louis Music Supply Company. It is obvious already that the University and the city live on intimate terms.

After two more residence halls and a home for the working girl, Chouteau House protrudes itself, a drab, humorless museum piece built in French Renaissance style during the 1880's by an eccentric prohibitionist. (Its owner couldn't stand kitchen odors so meals were prepared across the street in special servant quarters and carried to his table through a connecting tunnel.) This house of faded grandeur now echoes with the sounds of the University's student center. An abrupt architectural interruption, the famous Pius XII Memorial Library, was built next door between 1957 and 1959; its streamlined basic plan consists of three rectangles, one inside the other.

At the corner of Grand and West Pine, St. Louis University's future is the 22-acre vacant lot with the very tired, much-used Champlin Hall lingering alone on its northwest corner. Scheduled to disappear in 1967, the year before the University celebrates its 150th anniversary, Champlin Hall houses the drumbeaters and fund raisers who are collecting $46 million in a ten-year drive ending in 1968. Champlin Hall has weathered the changes in St. Louis and the University; it was once a girls' dormitory and before that a hotel with an unsavory reputation. A young woman, now on the University staff, recalled her arrival for her freshman year when she was assigned to the hall. She hailed a taxi at the train station and gave the address of Champlin Hall. The driver, who hadn't heard that the University had taken over the building as a dormitory, was shocked. She still remembers his admonition: "What's a nice girl like you want to go there for?"

In March, 1958, when the St. Louis Board of Aldermen acted to rejuvenate their city by approving the nation's most ambitious urban redevelopment plan, the Mill Creek Valley Project, the slum area next to the University was scheduled for clearance and the University had the opportunity to buy and build. One reason for the four-year delay between city action and University takeover was a suit brought by three members of POAU (Protestants

and Other Americans United for Separation of Church
and State). Finally, the Missouri Supreme Court upheld
a lower court ruling that the University paid a fair price,
was shown no favoritism and that the sale did not violate
the principle of separation of church and state. Once
again, city and University moved in tandem.

The network of buildings to be constructed on the
property will help to put a centralized roof over this
sprawling Jesuit enterprise in higher education. By 1964,
there will be the Busch Memorial Center, replacing
Chouteau House as a student union building, the Institute
of Technology, chemistry and physics buildings, a central utilities plant, a large classroom building, under-
ground lecture halls, and a soccer and softball field.

Caught in the whirl of image making and fund raising
necessary for any university which decides to meet the
challenge of rapidly rising enrollments, St. Louis University remains an unmistakably Jesuit institution with a
distinguished past, a well established present and a future
that has captured the imagination of city and University.
Said Father Jerome J. Marchetti, executive vice president: "We are out to make St. Louis the greatest Catholic University in the world and that includes being the
most complete." Thus emerges authentic Jesuit method-
ology behind the current bricks-and-mortar phase: a
physical identity for academic variety, appropriate means
for an ambitious end. At St. Louis, the argument is con-
vincingly presented that it is the foremost Catholic university in the country, taking into account quantity,
quality, and completeness of academic pursuits.

St. Louis University has almost 10,000 students pur-

suing the answers in 798 courses in 90 different fields.
Each June when about 1,700 degrees are awarded, they
are given in fields of study that extend to such specialties
as medical record library science, dietetics, radiologic
technology, meteorology, geophysical engineering, aero-
nautics and dental surgery. The School of Medicine has
graduated its first class of young doctors trained in nuclear medicine.

The educational enterprise is so extensive, so complicated and so deeply imbedded in St. Louis that it is
difficult to tell where the city ends and the University
begins. This results largely from the postwar growth
which squeezed the Institute of Technology into a converted mortuary and makes it necessary for students to
rush 16 blocks from liberal arts class on the North Campus (heart of the University and site of the 22-acre vacant lot) to the South campus for a biology or chemistry
class. A motorist stopping for a red light on Grand Avenue is liable to end up with a carload of coeds hitchhiking to their next class.

If you hang a map of Greater St. Louis on the wall and
throw darts at it, the odds are strongly in favor of hitting
a part of the city where the University is at work, study,
practice or play. If none of these, then a bulldozer may
be digging the foundations for another University project. As a Jesuit remarked, "Our campus is the community." He was referring to students practice teaching
in 45 St. Louis public schools, social service students assisting 25 social agencies, nursing students from the city's
hospitals, faculty members on civic committees, science
students who use the laboratories of local companies, law

students who assist lawyers defending indigent clients, and the city parks, fields and auditorium where University teams play.

Besides the North and South Campus located near the center of St. Louis, the University reaches across the river into Illinois where it operates the Parks College of Aeronautical Technology, the oldest federally approved aviation school in the United States. Parks College in East St. Louis became part of the University in 1946 (largely as a gift from its founder, Oliver Parks), joining ranks with the other academic units: College of Arts and Sciences, the Graduate School, Institute of Technology, and the Schools of Social Service, Medicine, Law, Dentistry, Commerce and Finance, Nursing and Health Services. Two other scattered units of the University train members of the Society of Jesus preparing for the priesthood. The School of Divinity in St. Mary's, Kansas, has the status of a Pontifical Institute of the Holy See; the College of Philosophy and Letters offers a program in philosophy on the main campus and a program in the humanities at Florissant, Missouri (where the Jesuits began their work in the St. Louis area by teaching Indians). A newly formed division, Metropolitan College, consolidates evening and adult education programs and all other community service programs not a part of the individual schools.

The consensus at St. Louis is that the University leads the Catholic field in philosophy and medicine and is the outstanding teacher-training institution. The Graduate School, which has 3,000 students working on advanced degrees, including 2,000 attending during the regular year and another 1,000 during the summer, is particularly strong in biochemistry, geophysics, political science and Latin-American studies.

One of its top-level administrators located the University in the United States academic pyramid by placing the handful of universities in the Harvard class at the peak and then ranking St. Louis among the first-rate universities, whether Catholic or secular. A recent recognition was inclusion in the Council of Graduate Schools in the United States. St. Louis was one of seven Catholic universities named as charter members; four of the seven are Jesuit institutions.

On the undergraduate level, St. Louis students have been on the move in the national competition for fellowships and scholarships. Between 1959 and 1961, they have won 26 Woodrow Wilson Fellowships, ranking second in the Catholic field nationally and second in their seven-state region among both Catholic and non-Catholic colleges. In 1961, there were four winners of Fulbright Fellowships and fourteen of National Science Foundation Fellowships in addition to eleven Woodrow Wilson winners. A total of 110 were in the college Honors Program for exceptional students, one of the first in the country when it was organized 24 years ago.

Only in a coed college can an exceptional student win academic honors and a wife, all in the same four years and in the same place, even in the same field of study. Charles M. Ankenbrandt of Cleveland met Marguerite Van Flandern of Cincinnati in their first year at St. Louis, "pinned" her in freshman year, proposed during their senior year and married her a week after graduation. A campus romance like many others, except that they were both physics majors graduating summa cum laude. Marguerite was the only member of the 1961 graduating class with a straight A record. Charles trailed behind. (He had one B on his record!) Each received a Woodrow Wilson Fellowship, Atomic Energy Commission and National Science Foundation Fellowships, and both began married life and pursuit of a Ph.D. in physics at the University of California.

The style and atmosphere of the University come from the College of Arts and Sciences with its 2,500 day and evening undergraduates. In the University's future planning, which calls for leveling off total enrollment at 15,000 by 1970, most of the 5,000 student increase will be on the undergraduate level. The present University enrollment, which comes from all 50 states and about sixty foreign countries, will then broaden to accommodate more boarding students from outside the immediate area. At present, two-thirds of the college students are from Greater St. Louis; about two out of three are Catholic and male.

One of the University's main attractions is a celebrated brand name: a Jesuit education. The Jesuit presence particularly dominates the college in the tradition of the "Ratio Studiorum," the remarkable educational bequest of St. Ignatius Loyola, founder of the Society of Jesus. The tradition calls for a stress on independent thinking, rather than passive acceptance of subject matter, as the Jesuits seek to turn out well rounded graduates with a strong moral commitment. The Jesuits inject ideals of excellence and independent thinking, the students add their feeling that they are at a superior institution, the city provides as a background its conservative, somewhat self-satisfied mentality. The result is a first impression that the students are smug. It upsets them to hear you say it.

Certainly, St. Louis does not have a rah-rah college. Besides the Jesuit attraction, the students enroll because it has a first-rate reputation and because, in many cases, it is local. For about two out of three students in the college, St. Louis was their first and only choice. Nationally, colleges find that about half of the students they accept never enroll, but three-quarters of the students accepted by St. Louis turn up for freshman registration. Moreover, Richard M. Keefe, dean of admissions, reports that the 1961 freshmen scored 25 percent higher in the American College Testing program than the national average. "An individual student is likely to find himself ranked lower in his class here than he would in the aggregate of the nation's freshman classes," he added.

In their sober, steadfast pursuit of a degree, the students go about their business without fanfare and regard it as bad taste to shout about their ideals or to be demonstrative. They are not out to change the world overnight, just to improve it by doing their job as well as possible. Propriety and politeness predominate, and students tend to look for faculty reactions as a guide when they face the issues of our times. When talking of students at secular colleges, St. Louis students note that the others are so involved in trying to resolve their own doubts that they can't push ahead in the learning process. St. Louis students shy away from the confusion of skepticism, and stress the solid intellectual basis provided by the Jesuits.

They feel order can be brought out of intellectual chaos, that the Jesuits have done so and that this is an academic warranty that they will do the same for the students. Intellectually, they feel it is presumptuous to fish before they learn to cut bait, to jump to opposing conclusions while they are still students.

When the intellectual independence of Jesuit teaching is thrust upon them, some become confused. The most talked-about course on campus is senior philosophy as taught by a salty Jesuit who heads the Philosophy Department, Father William Wade. He is dedicated to shaking the passivity out of his students by firing away at them with powerful arguments for the other philosophies besides the Thomistic philosophy which the Jesuits teach. As described by a Jesuit colleague, "Father Wade begins his course by announcing to the students: 'Father Wade is a Roman Catholic priest in good standing and he believes in the existence of God.' Then he proceeds to confuse the hell out of them. Students have come down to the dean's office in a panic after some of his classes." One can only add that the "Ratio Studiorum" has a home along the Mississippi.

The students are much like soldiers turned loose in a wilderness as part of their basic training. They have a compass, limited supplies and their own personal resources. Deep down they know that if they get completely lost, a search party will come after them, though meanwhile the feeling of being lost can be uncomfortable. To them college is not so much an adventure of the mind as an exercise and training of the intellect.

In a revealing bull session, a group of St. Louis stu-

dents tried to explain themselves and in their attempt
revealed much about their college in particular and, possibly, about Catholic college students in general. After
rejecting the descriptive adjective, smug (one coed
said, "Why use a derogatory term? Why not say proud
of what we have here?"), they discussed the "typical"
student.

Said one coed, planning to go into social service:
"Around here, it is difficult to describe a typical student.
We have such a cross-section. But I think the most typical way I can describe him is that first of all he is concerned about religion. Next he is concerned about what
he is going to do with himself. Next you will find a lot
of people concerned with what they can do to contribute,
here and now, to some effort on campus, in the community, anywhere. I would say the typical student doesn't
work his utmost for his courses. He's usually involved
in one school activity on the side. He is much more serious than students I know in Big Ten universities. He
doesn't look only to the next beer party. He thinks of
life in general, not just to the immediate future. He does
most of his work, and I guess a little beyond that."

A senior active in student government: "I don't think
there is a typical student. There may be two different
kinds of students. There are students who are here to
pass the time away because their fathers have enough
money and those going to college specifically in order to
get a better job. This is one category. The second would
be the student trying to better himself as a person. I
think there is a great cleavage between the two types.
Not that the abilities or natural talent of either type is

greater than the other, but the outlook is so different. I think you will find this in any college. I often wonder whether we have the right to deny a place in a school for a person who is there primarily for the social aspects. I think a university is a mixture of typical people according to what they want."

A junior who is a history major: "I think there are three different types of students here. There are those who are here to catch a husband, those who are here to keep out of the draft and there are those here to get an education. I think after the first year or year and a half, the former two are not around anymore. So you are left with only those here to get an education. Perhaps they keep grades in mind because they know when they get out grades will get them a better job. And the better job you have the more responsible position you have, both in your business life and in the community itself. I think our students here realize this. They are the mature minds we have here on campus."

A junior active on the school newspaper: "I think the typical student here is rather concerned with appearances and watches other students to see not only the way they dress but the way they think. We had a newspaper poll about what students want in marriage. The girls wanted an intelligent, handsome fellow. The guys wanted a beautiful girl who is a good mixer, who knew how to dress. . . ."

At this point, the two coeds present rose in anger. One said sharply that she knew two of the girls interviewed very well and knew the kind of husband they want. "They're not nearly so flighty," she said. "It's just they don't want it down in print for everyone to laugh at."

To which the school newspaperman replied: "What kind of a culture do we have around school if you can't express what you really feel. . . . But that isn't my main point. I think the typical student is what Eliot would call the hollow man. Or Dante would put him in the circle of Hell among those who can't choose."

From there the discussion went into intellectual attitudes. The students described as "presumptuous" one student who had rejected Thomistic philosophy. ("How could he have studied enough philosophies to make a choice?") There were several references to intellectual humility while still learning, respect for the learning of their professors, hesitation in the face of any extreme. They sounded older than they looked.

Since most students commute to school from St. Louis, college has not produced an abrupt change in their lives. They retain neighborhood friends, remain within the family circle, and they can manage college at a reasonable cost. In the College of Arts and Sciences, for instance, tuition is only $400 per semester. This produces a student body ranging from those who earn all expenses while living at home to out-of-town students whose families can afford to send them away to college. The result is a microcosm of the city in the student body.

Practically all students work part time, adding another distraction to college life, but also discouraging ivory tower attitudes. Some even work full time. The students have all the usual part-time jobs and some unlikely ones: banana price checker in a warehouse, fur tester, cattle buyer, tutor for the youngsters in a touring company of

The Music Man, driving a horse-drawn carriage around St. Louis' Forest Park, washing special laboratory glassware in the Medical School, and playing, in season, Santa Claus or Easter Bunny.

In the school newspaper, the students demonstrate a lively and literate interest in University affairs, particularly on the editorial page with editorials, columns, and letters to the editor. Though far from cosmic in subject matter, student letters are outspoken. In one issue, for instance, student letters dissected the college coed, criticized shortening of library hours and the way coeds dress when they are not going to church or on a date, praised modification of dormitory hours, defended the custom of "pinning."

The school's coeds are a natural object of interest and comment, but there is every indication that the University takes them in stride. The campus intellectuals talk condescendingly of "campus cookies" whose main concerns are bridge (for some students an obsession), cokes in the student union and dates. But by all accounts, the coeds appreciate the chance to attend a Jesuit university and soon adjust to the fact that they must work hard to stay afloat academically. It also helps to have dates close at hand, though slight complications are inevitable, such as the night one student didn't know his dormitory was having a dance in the lounge. He breezed into the lounge in his red pajamas and was practically on the dance floor before he escaped.

This kind of contretemps appeals to St. Louis students. It is homey, unaffected, mildly amusing; the victim is wounded only slightly in his dignity. Or students delight over the conflict with authority involving the animal lovers in Walsh Hall, a men's dormitory. The students had acquired various birds, snakes, baby alligators and one basset hound on loan from the University of Missouri. A crisis arose when a dormitory counselor stumbled over a one-and-a-half-foot boa constrictor, provoking the following official notice on the bulletin board, its undertone of mock seriousness indicative of the balance in the St. Louis mentality: "No animals are allowed in the dormitories. This includes dogs, cats, boa constrictors, and all other creatures which fly through the air, creep along the earth or bore into it. If you wish to save them from extermination, send them home for safekeeping. All animals found in the dormitory will be used for dissecting or be removed from circulation in other ways which are equally effective."

The highlight of the student year, Sadie Hawkins Day, personifies the down-to-earth attitude at St. Louis. It is a day beginning with a parade of decorated cars and floats in a takeoff of the Veiled Prophet Ball, the fashionable event that opens the city's social season. A foot race follows in which "eligible unmarried females chase eligible unmarried males." Coeds who run fast enough and boys who don't then have a mock marriage ceremony on the miniscule lawn in front of Chouteau House (very little greenery is visible anywhere at the university). The evening's dance is not presided over by a campus queen, in full stereotyped coed bliss, but by "Sadie Hawkins." She crowns the Kampus King, who is elected after campaigning the way he would in Dogpatch.

The cosmic side of St. Louis University is illustrated

by its involvement in the space age. Several hundred
alumni employed by McDonnell Aircraft, both in St.
Louis and at Cape Canaveral, shared in the success of
America's first astronaut. More than 125 McDonnell engineers were attending evening courses at the Institute
of Technology to keep up with the latest scientific ad-
vances. The Medical School was involved in space research, the law school in Comparative Air Law taught by
NATO visiting professor Peter Lodrup from the University of Oslo. Parks College of Aeronautical Technology held a symposium on outer space, the Institute of
Technology was analyzing data received from weather
satellites.

To meet the variety of its academic needs, St. Louis
University has recruited faculty across religious lines.
It is well beyond the stage of a faculty dominated by
laymen; many of the laymen are not Catholic. Out of a
full-time and part-time faculty of about 1,250, about
one-third are not Catholics. They include 85 Jews, 54
Presbyterians, and 42 Methodists, as well as Lutherans,
Congregationalists, Episcopalians, and Baptists.

A random sampling of the academic figures assembled
on campus must include Dr. Kurt von Schuschnigg, the
scholarly chancellor of Austria who defied Hitler, Dr.
Edward A. Doisy, Sr., who won the Nobel Prize for his
work on Vitamin K, Dr. Thomas Neill and Dr. James
Collins, respectively historian and philosopher with national reputations. Father Walter J. Ong, the English
professor and social commentator, whom a colleague described as "one of the ten most quoted men in American

academic circles," spent the 1961–1962 school year as a fellow at Wesleyan University's Center for Advanced Studies. Father Leo C. Brown, nationally known labor arbitrator, was named by President Kennedy to head an emergency board in a major airline labor dispute.

Numerically, the Jesuits are in the minority at St. Louis University. They are only about a hundred in a full-time faculty of 450 and a half dozen in a part-time faculty of 800, but the Jesuit presence dominates and their authority is unquestioned. A student illustrated the Jesuit role on campus by recalling a snowball fight involving some 400 students from adjacent dormitories. The scene of battle was West Pine Boulevard, thereby tying up city traffic and bringing four police cars to the scene. When the police got out of their cars and ordered the boys to stop, they were showered with snowballs. Soon after this point of maximum chaos, a solitary Jesuit appeared and shouted, "O.K. boys that's enough. Stop." And all stopped immediately.

Jesuit control of the total enterprise was underlined on December 16, 1961, when the dean of the Medical School, Dr. James W. Colbert, Jr., was dismissed in an incident which received national attention. One of the strongest personalities at the University and medical dean for eight years since his appointment at the age of thirty-three, Dr. Colbert became involved in a controversy concerning part-time faculty members at the Medical School. The dean fired two veteran professors who had denounced his action in dismissing 149 part-time faculty members for refusing "to accept their educational re-

sponsibilities when assigned." *The New York Times*
called it "one of the most serious policy controversies"
in the history of the University.

Father Marchetti, who, as executive vice president is
the key man in day-to-day operation of the University,
refers to "a great learning process in which Jesuits and
laymen are learning to work in partnership." Undoubtedly, the University has made considerable progress in
this learning process and the present administration is
characterized by realism, friendliness and good will. Possibly one indication of the progress is the open discussion
of whether Jesuits get preference in dealing with the administration. The Jesuits deny this; in fact, some claim
that the administration leans over backwards to keep its
lay faculty happy. Father Marchetti emphasizes that
"once a Jesuit walks through the cloister door, he's on
his own in the University." Not all lay faculty members
would agree; one claimed that their lack of power creates
a "civil service mentality," though no one at St. Louis
seemed intimidated or hesitant to discuss, comment and
criticize.

Amid an array of exciting academics who seem appropriately collected on a Jesuit campus, there is one
figure whose image dominates and whose single voice
summarizes the get-up-and-go of the University. He is
the school's president, Father Paul C. Reinert, a leading
figure in United States higher education and the most indefatigable man on campus. (He even bats clean-up in
the annual softball game between Jesuit and lay faculty.)
By every standard, St. Louis has a president worthy of
its past and remarkably suited to its expansionist present

and future. One well traveled Jesuit said of Father Reinert: "I have been in 26 Jesuit provinces all over the
world—some, of course, only overnight—and he is the
biggest thing I have ever seen in a Jesuit uniform. If you
need a general, he would be the best man you could
pick."

In keeping with the enlarged role of the University,
Father Reinert has city, regional and national involvements. He has been president of the accrediting agency
for 400 colleges and universities and 3,400 high schools
in a 19-state Middle West area. He was named to President Eisenhower's Committee on Education Beyond the
High School and was a delegate to the 1955 White House
Conference on Education as well as a member of the
13-man educational advisory group of the International
Cooperation Administration. In 1957, he was cochair-
man of Missouri's State Commission on Higher Education. He is an adviser to the government on programs in
higher education and he was one of 28 college presidents
called upon to discuss the Peace Corps with its director.
The Jesuits elected him chairman of the Conference of
Presidents of Jesuit Colleges and Universities, while both
the Catholic Interracial Council of St. Louis and B'nai
B'rith honored him for bettering group relations. For
good measure, he was chairman and is still a member of
the commission directing educational television in St.
Louis.

When he is not logging some 50,000 air miles a year
meeting alumni and spearheading the fund-raising drive,
Father Reinert puts in what is reputed to be an 80-hour
week. He is on the job from 8:30 A.M. (after a 5 A.M.

rising, an hour of meditation, celebration of Mass, reading his breviary, and breakfast) until 10 or 11 at night. When the opportunity arises, usually at University functions, he revels in athletic competition topped off by a long swim. Faculty members who have played opposite him describe Father Reinert as a "fiercely competitive athlete." Despite his fondness for sports, one of his first moves as president was to drop intercollegiate football. The reasons were the same as those given by other universities: the expense and the possible compromise of academic standards. (Basketball is the school's top spectator sport, though soccer has been a surprise. In its first two years of collegiate competition, the University drew on talent developed in the city, where soccer is a popular sandlot game, and became national champion in 1959 and 1960.)

Now in his early fifties, Father Reinert still brings to his various roles incredible physical energy that is almost alarming, academic renown and outstanding credentials, including a Ph.D. in educational administration from the University of Chicago, and a hale and hearty personality. He is not high-powered in his manner; he can charm, impress and relax a visitor at the same time. He is neither covered with ivy nor with the slick veneer of stereotyped educators. It is not surprising that he was nicknamed the "student's president" for his informal manner and personal interest in students. As a Catholic educator, he is against intellectual ghettos and parochial smugness. "Beyond the certainties of faith," he emphasizes, "we are scrambling for truth like anyone else."

In 1961 he gave the American Council on Education

a sample of his characteristic straight talk and common sense as he made it clear that he is not letting anyone lose sight of a university's goal and its president's responsibilities. He told 1,800 college and university presidents meeting in Washington: "They [the students] wonder about the wisdom of status-seeking college presidents who authorize thousands for monumental structures and only hundreds for library books; thousands for facilities for a few athletes and little or nothing for the faceless thousands of students who are the fans in the stands; millions for bricks and mortar and relatively little for warm-hearted men and women who will listen and understand."

When Father Reinert became president in 1949 at the age of thirty-eight, St. Louis was an important regional university with national prestige only in certain academic areas, especially medicine. Even its graduates tended to identify with a specific school in the university rather than with the entire university. In downtown St. Louis, an alumnus would tend to say that he was a graduate of Finance or Arts rather than a graduate of St. Louis University. A newcomer had trouble finding the University for its scattered parts; it was growing like the city: getting bigger, more complicated, more unwieldy, and slightly threadbare.

In 1958 when the University committed itself to both expansion and consolidation as part of the development plans, its image began to grow by design and by merit. The St. Louis *Post-Dispatch*, the city's conscience, editorialized in April, 1959: "By extending its overcrowded campus to the east of Grand Avenue, the University can improve its facilities for technological and scientific education and prepare for the larger enrollments ahead. It can also make a substantial contribution to the improvement of what is now a sadly blighted neighborhood. . . . So the community should be grateful that St. Louis decided some years ago not to abandon its present location. And it should be eager to help the University to enlarge and improve its campus." The mayor of St. Louis, Raymond R. Tucker, agreed; he said the University's expansion program "will mean a rebirth of our mid-city."

Drawing on the University's community acceptance, Father Reinert formed a President's Council composed of ninety of the city's leading business and civic leaders. Its ranks included chairmen of the board, presidents and vice presidents from some of St. Louis' and America's leading firms: Canada Dry Bottling, Missouri Pacific Railroad, Universal Match Corporation, Wabash Railroad, Pet Milk, Monsanto Chemical, Southwestern Bell Telephone, International Shoe and Western Publishing. Two of the most helpful have been Falstaff Brewing Company and Anheuser-Busch (St. Louis has the largest brewery in the world). The new student union building will be named after the grandfather, father and brother of August A. Busch, Jr., who is general chairman of the University's development drive. A new 17-story men's residence, Griesedieck Memorial Hall, is named after the late head of Falstaff Brewing.

Projecting itself nationally, the University has made its platforms available to a wide range of renowned speakers. In the course of 1961, guest speakers included Dr.

William C. Menninger of the Menninger Foundation, Norman St. John-Stevas, English author and barrister, and Rear Admiral Edward C. Kenny, the Navy's surgeon general, in addition to prominent figures in the arts, geology, mathematics, weather, classical languages. The highlight of 1961 was the annual Founders Week celebration marking the University's 143rd anniversary. Campus workshops were held for alumni, faculty and community leaders on a variety of problems—the space age, professionalism in engineering, pornography and the law, professional education for business. Henry Cabot Lodge, former United States Ambassador to the United Nations, spoke at the Civic Dinner held during Founders Week. Assistant Secretary of State Harlan Cleveland, speaking at the faculty dinner the same week, launched an important proposal of the Kennedy Administration to extend international law to outer space.

On the local level, the University, through its Metropolitan College, provides college-level courses over television. The school's involvement with broadcasting goes back to 1912 when it established the first university station in the world. One of its most successful TV adventures has been a weekly series on Communism, presented by the University's new Institute on Communism and Freedom. Established to provide a sound academic approach to Communism and the principles of freedom, the Institute holds summer workshops for area high school teachers. Other high school teachers attend refresher courses in order to stay up to date on their specialties.

From its early days, the University has been committed

to serving immediate, local needs; its wider involvements have developed from this secure base of operations. The school was founded, in the first place, by
diocesan priests as an "academy for young gentlemen" in
a one-story house on the riverfront. At the time, St.
Louis was a frontier town of 3,000. The Jesuits arrived
on the scene in 1824 by opening a school for Indian
boys in Florissant, Missouri, and the Jesuit name soon
attracted attention. (Before the United States came
into being, there were more than 700 Jesuit universities
and colleges throughout the world.)

According to one historical account: "A few of the
most respectable white families of St. Louis sent their
sons to the 'Indian Seminary,' for want of better ac-
commodations. About the same time a desire was generally expressed among the people of St. Louis and
throughout the state of Missouri that the Jesuit fathers
should not confine their efforts to the Indians, among
whom little good was likely to be effected, but should
open a college in St. Louis." One of the "respectable
white" students at the "Indian Seminary" was Charles
Pierre Chouteau, a great-grandson of Pierre Laclede, the
founder of St. Louis.

As negotiations for adoption of St. Louis College by
the Jesuits went on, a shortage of instructors forced the
school to suspend operations in 1827. When the Jesuits
agreed to staff the college, ground was broken in 1828
for a three-story building on a city lot donated for a
Catholic college. The college was formally opened on
November 2, 1829, and within a few weeks 150 students
were enrolled. On December 28, 1832, it became St.

Louis University. Since Washington University, the city's only other university, did not open until 1853, the Jesuit school has become almost as much a landmark as the Mississippi.

An interesting footnote to the University's current prestige in the field of medicine is the fact that in 1855 the University and its Medical School severed connections in the face of difficulties caused by the Know-Nothing Movement. Medical education did not return to the University until 1902; today it has the largest Catholic medical center in the world. About a mile south of the main campus, the schools of Medicine, Dentistry, and Nursing and Health Services are grouped around Firmin Desloge, a teaching hospital, Cardinal Glennon Memorial Hospital for Children and the newly completed David P. Wohl Memorial Health Institute. Including the other teaching hospitals, St. Mary's and Mount St. Rose, the university group of hospitals served 37,500 patients in 1961. Cardinal Glennon and Firmin Desloge hospitals handled a quarter of a million persons in their outpatient departments.

The most celebrated new building at St. Louis University is the Pius XII Memorial Library, the only structure designated by the late pontiff as a personal memorial. The $4.25 million library which houses most of the University's more than 600,000 volumes, achieved international renown with its microfilmed copies of the handwritten books of the Vatican Library. This has placed at the disposal of American scholars the richest manuscript collection in the world—11 million handwritten pages now available on 873,000 feet of film. The collection of

writings from the fifth to the nineteenth centuries was
described by an Oxford scholar as the "most important
single addition ever made to the libraries of America."
In a cooperative project with Brandeis University, St.
Louis is microfilming the Hebrew manuscripts in the
Vatican Library to supplement the Greek, Latin and
Western language manuscripts in the collection.

Father Lowrie J. Daly, a history professor, originated
the $350,000 microfilm project, which was financed by
the Knights of Columbus. The collection, which still
has not been catalogued by scholars, is a primary source
for research on the development of Western thought. It
also contains surprises. One professor has discovered—
in his pursuit of manuscripts on mathematics—ninth-
century recipes for filet of sole, fifteenth-century Latin
joke books, Egyptian papyri, and the love letters of
Henry VIII to Anne Boleyn. The library also has priceless collections of rare books, the archives of the Missouri Province of the Jesuits, the St. Louis Archdiocesan
Archives and Jesuitica Americana. The latter, 900,000
microfilmed pages on the Jesuits in America, led to establishment at St. Louis of the only branch of the Jesuit Historical Institute outside Rome.

Air-conditioned, well lighted, its books easily accessi-
ble on open shelves, the library has attracted the students
in multiplying numbers since its doors were opened on
May 18, 1959. Use of the central library doubled in the
first year and doubled again in the second year since mov-
ing from its grim quarters in overcrowded Du Bourg
Hall. (At the time the books were being moved, a laborer
was heard to say: "They built a new library. You'd

think they'd buy new books.") The Lindell Plaza of the library is dominated by a statue executed by Ivan Mestrovic of Pope Pius XII with his right hand raised in the teaching gesture. It faces the Masonic temples across the street.

With so much on the drawing board, in the works and already accomplished in so many directions, a momentary flashback to a May 6, 1837, meeting of the University's board of trustees shows a long-standing determination to stay up to date at St. Louis. After setting down the requirements of a classical education, the trustees added in 1837: "But this preeminence of the ancient classics does not imply a depreciation of any science or any branch of education which, in its own proper sphere, promotes the welfare of human society."

Or as Father Reinert states it: "We are attempting to build up an institution which involves highly trained faculty and capable students in order to pursue the intellectual life in as broad a number of fields as we can do adequately. We want to produce graduates as well or better trained than those from other institutions and at the same time equally well developed from both practical and intellectual viewpoints in their faith and its relationship to their individual lives."

ROSARY COLLEGE

Beauty and the Books

As GRADUATON approaches at Rosary College near Chicago, the outgoing and incoming seniors engage in a sunset ceremony that symbolizes more than is intended. The graduating seniors, in academic caps and gowns, carry lighted candles in a procession, flanked by the juniors who wear formal dresses and carry long-stemmed red roses. The setting sun casts a sentimental graduation glow as the seniors exchange the symbol of truth for the symbol of charity.

These *veritas* and *caritas* symbols, which appear on the college's shield, have a more prosaic and practical significance. The candle suggests the midnight oil which the new seniors talk about burning in order to graduate from this outstanding Catholic liberal arts women's college.

The rose must have something to do with beauty, considering the marriage rate of Rosary graduates. More than 80 percent of all who graduated in the 1950's are married; so were one-third of the class of 1960 about a year after graduation.

Both the reputation and the distinctive character of Rosary College stem from the compatibility of the candle and the rose: the serious pursuit of an education now and a husband later. From the tables of the students' dining room to the president's office, a liberal arts education is described at Rosary as an invaluable end in itself, producing young women well equipped to succeed in any career, marriage included. Rejecting both narrow vocational training and the finishing school approach, the Rosary nuns self-consciously maintain a tradition begun in 1848 at Sinsinawa Female Academy in Wisconsin when the usual curriculum of "seminaries for young girls" was ignored. The Dominican Sisters of Sinsinawa taught their young girls astronomy, logic, history, and natural philosophy.

Later, it became St. Clara Academy and College before changing its name and location in 1922 at the invitation of Cardinal Mundelein, then Archbishop. In establishing Rosary College in River Forest, Illinois, the Dominican Sisters set about fulfilling Cardinal Mundelein's "hope that this will be the Catholic Vassar of the Middle West." The consensus at Rosary and in the surrounding area is that the sisters are succeeeding. A newly hired English professor, a non-Catholic, found on inquiring about the school that it is often described as "the best girls' college in the Chicago area."

At Rosary, a liberal arts education is practically an obsession and the last visitor who tried to talk the College's president into introducing a physical therapy department left muttering under his breath. "My faculty just wouldn't stand for it," Sister Mary Aurelia, the president, said. "We are firmly convinced that our main reason for being is to provide young women with a Christian education. The best preparation a young person can have for living as well as making a living is in the liberal arts tradition."

But it is an intangible goal, as significant as girls studying in the library late on a Friday afternoon and as unspectacular. Rosary is best described as some 900 young ladies in pursuit of an education, led, egged on, and prodded by a first-rate faculty of 56 Dominican nuns, 13 laywomen, ten laymen, and three Dominican priests. The pursuit—sometimes the girls complain that it feels like a forced march—takes place on a 30-acre Gothic-flavored campus ten miles from Chicago's boisterous Loop.

The school's newspaper, the *Rosarian*, reminded prospective graduates in one issue: "One of the grimmest memories you will have after graduation from Rosary will be the times you sacrificed a night's sleep and a year's health for daily languages assignments, clearance history tests cramming and required term papers." A report on Rosary at examination time produced the following items: One girl cramming in a linen closet with a sign taped on the door, "Let me know if anything happens." Two freshmen discussing an English composition test, "Don't tell me that there's a difference between erratic and erotic." One girl had her exam-week schedule drawn like a battle plan in five different colors.

Across the gap of generations, the faculty and students at Rosary are trying to talk to each other and, while they may not succeed at first, contact is apparently made by junior and senior years. It is then that the Rosary products emerge: serious young ladies talking of values and commitments, term papers and dates, a job, marriage, and a family. But they don't talk of shooting for the stars. As one junior said, echoing what was said in many different ways by her fellow students: "You must try to do the best you can. You can't be more daring than that."

While some students complain of severe restrictions and a limited horizon at Rosary, most agree that the College is less restrictive than the typical Catholic girls' college and they are enthusiastic about the nuns. The alumnae director, a Rosary graduate, cited the "unusual degree of freedom" granted the girls. There is no assembly roll call, no compulsory Mass; the girls are expected to demonstrate maturity and individual responsibility. She cited a spirit of individuality permeating both the religious order and their College.

Actually, the Dominican Sisters at Rosary seem more daring than the students. For instance, they are regarded as politically more liberal than the girls, though this is not to suggest that any conservative wave has swept the campus. When a newly formed Conservative Club called its first meeting in search of members, only six students turned up and it was impossible to find a faculty moderator in tune with their views. Thus it was no surprise that Kennedy defeated Nixon, 261 to 81, in a student poll,

though cries of ballot stuffing were heard in the dormitories.

When the local American Legion post protested the
school's presentation of *The Crucible*—Arthur Miller's
controversial play about witch-hunts that was generally
interpreted as an attack on the methods of the late Senator McCarthy—the show went on anyhow. At one
point, several years ago, the Chicago *Tribune*, citadel of
Midwestern conservatism, lumped together Chicago University, Roosevelt University and Rosary as "hotbeds of
liberalism." (In 1961, the *Tribune* included Rosary in its
survey of twenty of the best liberal arts colleges in the
Midwest.)

For several years, the students in "Twentieth Century
American Capitalism" have held an annual mock trial of
Alger Hiss. The trial is set up to determine the degree to
which Hiss was guilty as found and to consider whether
the trial fairly represented the case. For technical advice,
the students turn to fathers who are lawyers. The trial
is also organized to point up the Communist controversies of the 1940's.

As on most campuses, J. D. Salinger has been the literary craze. The college library had a long waiting list
for his best-seller, *Franny and Zooey*, and the campus
paperback store, called "The Pit," had trouble meeting
the demand for *Catcher in the Rye*. When the father of
one of the students noticed his daughter reading the latter and asked if the good sisters knew that she is reading
it, the girl reported the remark to a nun, who replied
jokingly, "There is nothing there that isn't in the Bible."
The next time the student went home and told her father,

the nun reported—with a twinkle—the father said: "You ask sister, 'Where in the Bible?' "

The Rosary nuns, rather than abdicate their responsibilities, seem so wholeheartedly committed to the process of education that they concentrate on teaching and leading rather than telling and dictating. As the college dean, Sister Mary Fredericus, noted, "All we can do is teach principles and make them as clear, realistic and attractive as possible." There are no signs that the nuns at Rosary are running from the world, and they don't encourage their students to do so. For instance, the faculty sent a letter to Martin Luther King supporting "nonviolent action against the evils and injustice of racial bias and segregation." One week the Chicago press ran a picture of a Rosary nun at a luncheon with Bette Davis, the next another nun with Ralph Bunche at a conference. The Rosary nuns travel from Dallas to New York for professional conferences and meetings; they write poems, critical reviews, books. They convey a mood of involvement as well as commitment.

Sister Mary Gregory, chairman of the Speech Department, who became something of a celebrity in 1959 when she acted as technical advisor for *The Sound of Music*, emphasized the absence of "spoon-feeding" at Rosary and pointed out that students not seriously interested in an education are soon weeded out. "We are trying to teach the students to think for themselves," she added. As for the sister-professors themselves, she pointed to the coordination, rather than conflict, of their roles as religious and as teachers. The Sinsinawa Dominicans joined the order to be both.

As in any liberal arts college, the real business of education is carried on, day in, day out, in the daily classroom encounters between teacher and student. When mixed properly, the result is education, and the Dominican nuns, with an air of professional modesty, are the first to say that they can always improve the mixture. This pursuit of improvement, rather than a blind attitude that all is well, is a persistent piece of evidence that Rosary deserves its academic reputation.

Having set the process of give-and-take in motion, the Rosary nuns have had to face student complaints that they are not having enough classroom discussions. This erupted into a series of letters published in the school newspaper, in itself an indication that the nuns were achieving some success. Wrote one student: "There are teachers who, for various obscure reasons, refuse to accept or even listen to student opinions. . . . Teachers are here not only to teach, but to listen and help. Students should cooperate in this two-way education." Another presented, Gripe 1, that there should be student-teacher exchange beyond the lectures, and Gripe 2, that there is too much "busy work" and not enough time "to benefit from the culture that is seeping about the hallowed halls."

When faced with such complaints, the Rosary nuns don't wave the stick of authority or engage in aggressive apologetics. They engage in critical self-examination. In discussing Rosary with them you come away with the feeling (which most, but not all, students confirm) that the message has got through to the students that the Rosary nuns are eager to hear their ideas, want to treat them as mature young ladies and are the first to applaud the clash of ideas that makes teaching interesting.

In one freshman logic course, the students were wrestling with some up-to-date applications of their subject
matter. On a mimeographed sheet under the heading,
"Syllogisms and Their Variations," they were asked to
consider such statements as "Mr. Y is organizing a strike.
He must be a Red," or "One who would exclude Orientals from the U.S. is a materialist." In facing the question of whether a Negro is deprived of his rights if you
refuse to sell him your home, the discussion reached a
lively pitch. It brought one girl's frank admission, "I feel
one way intellectually, and another way emotionally."
Then came the nun's reply, the soft-spoken battle cry
of the Rosary faculty: "Part of growing up is to make
our emotions agree with our intellect."

In Rosary's circumscribed world of women, the student body can be separated in more ways than one, into
freshmen, sophomores, juniors and seniors. It is a surprise to discover just how much they differ in mentality
and frame of mind. Though the following generalizations are probably more applicable to the 356 boarding
students than to the 512 commuters, they summarize the
journey from teenager to young lady at Rosary College
as described by both students and faculty.

Freshmen— Still dazed by the transition from high
school to college, they live somewhere between the two
levels of education. They are immersed in the struggle to
survive academically, to find their place in the school,
and to get a date with a Notre Dame man.

Sophomore— The most troubled, interesting and con-

fused members of the student body, they are experienc-
ing what is known nationally as the "sophomore slump."
They are making up their minds about staying in the
environment of a girls' college, entertaining second
thoughts about Rosary, struggling with the choice of a
major field of study, which they must make by the end
of the year. About 68 percent of the freshmen return for
sophomore year and 75 percent of the sophomores return
for junior year.

Juniors— The academic decisions made, their commitment to Rosary solidified, the juniors seem to grow up
during the alchemy of a single summer vacation. They
leave in June as girls and return in September as young
ladies. Recalling her sophomore unrest, one pretty bru-
nette, dressed for a Friday date, said: "Last year when I
was a sophomore I swore I would never come back to
Rosary. Then somehow I decided to return. It was the
best decision I ever made and I will certainly send my
daughter here." Another junior added, "The thing about
Rosary is that the nuns treat you like an adult and they
are terrific teachers." Not surprisingly, better than nine
out of ten juniors return for senior year.

Seniors— One eye on graduation, the seniors talk of
gratitude for what Rosary has given them and of a realization that education will make them better persons,
wives, mothers. They are concerned about harmony in
the college as someday they will be concerned about harmony in the community. They are very serious as only
young ladies can be and they become indignant if anyone
questions the value of sending a girl to college. They are
getting ready to exchange the candle for the rose.

Looking back over the years, Sister Mary Thomasine, the stimulating economics professor whose class holds the mock trial of Alger Hiss, described the changing attitudes of the Rosary students. It may sum up students at other Catholic girls' colleges as well. Sister Thomasine recalled the girl of the 1920's for whom college was a privilege and who stressed cultural improvement. She had less contact with the outside world than the student of the thirties who began to think in terms of service, a desire accentuated during the 1940's by the war. In the 1950's, idealism declined and the students sought a conformist atmosphere. "They were afraid to commit themselves," she noted. "They were female versions of the organization man, playing it cool, not highly committed." With the growing accent on grades and the pursuit of fellowships, the student of the 1950's sought to promote personal goals. Sister Thomasine finds the students of the 1960's regaining a desire to serve "without feeling silly." Their horizons extend beyond the kitchen and the nursery, while not abandoning either as their basic roles. They have an interest in service overseas and a determination to operate on an intelligent level even as suburban housewives. Nonetheless, as a whole the postwar generation "lacks energy and is incapable of sustained ardor," Sister Thomasine observes. Part of the problem has an obvious origin—they are not as active physically as previous generations. "They get their grades and will be good people, but they won't be great," Sister Thomasine adds wistfully. The Rosary sisters prefer to aim at the stars.

While it is difficult for a male intruder, separated by

time, place and experience, to infiltrate this female environment, a running column on what "Rosarians Are Talking About" has been provided by a young lady named Judy Colohan who is a cousin of the wry comedian Bob Newhart. While she admits that half her items are completely made up because "conversation in the Grill runs from last weekend to next weekend," the popularity of her column in the school paper indicates that she is a dependable barometer of student life. Here are samples: October—"Rosarians are talking about the values prevalent on the Rosary campus, or the lack of them . . . hedge-hopping to get into the [new] Residence Hall . . . the alumnae brunch . . . India and Indians . . . new paint in the smoker . . . canvassing . . . football games . . . October devotions." November—"Rosarians are talking about U.S. prestige, its ups and downs . . . Marcel Marceau and Handel's 'Messiah,' a week apart . . . Christmas jobs or the lack of them . . . Faculty-Student dinners . . . jet planes cleaning their landing gear on the roof every five minutes [en route to O'Hare Airport]." December—"Rosarians are talking about increase in drinking problems in the U.S. . . . The Robert Shaw Chorale . . . spring, a little early . . . the end of an era . . . Clark Gable . . . next semester's schedule, akin to working jigsaw puzzles blindfolded . . . window wonderland in the Loop . . . colds." February—"Rosarians are talking about Africa . . . skating parties . . . missioning from Albuquerque to Brazil . . . grad schools . . . the Jackie Kennedy look, as interpreted by late risers with an 8:30 class . . . the bright colors in the ceramics lab these days . . . tired blood, if any." March—"Rosarians are talking about Sunday afternoon socials at Notre Dame . . . proposed theology department tea with virtues on the right, passions on the left . . . tax refunds." April—"Rosarians are talking about the Steamboat Stompers—music to break a leg by. They were really great to listen to, but dancing? . . . research papers, the end of many a thought of grad school . . . folk singing, sign of the 'in' group." May—"Rosarians are talking about the tea circuit . . . weight increases . . . May crowning, foiled again by the weather. . . ."

By the time Rosary students graduate, they have built their education on a liberal arts base of required courses, including English literature, philosophy, theology, history and a foreign language. They have studied the Bible, traveled through *The Odyssey* and visited Heaven, Hell and Purgatory in *The Divine Comedy*. They have also taken a special marriage course, taught by a priest and focused on a subject that grows in importance as graduation approaches. The final two years center on a major field of study in philosophy, the humanities, the natural and social sciences or mathematics. Particularly noteworthy are majors in English, foreign languages (including Portuguese and Russian), history, art, mathematics and chemistry. These major fields tend to produce the most students who go on to do graduate work. For instance, out of 51 chemistry graduates in a ten-year period, five went on to study for Ph.D.'s, four for M.D.'s and seven for master's degrees. Overall, about 15 percent of each graduating class go on to graduate school.

Home economics, the only visibly vocational major in

the program, is carefully weighted with liberal arts and science requirements, steered away from the cookbook and toward the textbook. While there is no education major, enough education credits are offered to meet elementary and high school teaching requirements. Almost half of the recent graduates have taken teaching jobs, though a growing number are being attracted by government jobs. In addition, the nuns inspire a steady stream of religious vocations. Between 1952 and 1961, there were 78 Rosary vocations for the Sinsinawa Dominicans and 35 for other communities, with three out of four persevering in their vocations.

The Rosary nuns carry on their educational enterprise in a dignified network of buildings centered around the impressive cloistered walk of Massachelli Hall, named after the young Italian missionary who founded the Sinsinawa order and established their teaching tradition. The modest expansion of the past decade reflects their point of view. In 1952 it was a new Fine Arts Building, in 1958 an addition to the science building, in 1961, a new residence hall built with a federal loan. Next on the agenda is an extension to the library. The guiding principle, the nuns point out, is how to make bricks and mortar serve teaching and learning. As far as the sisters are concerned, the present plant can serve about 1,000 students properly, and that is as large a student body as they envisage.

Rosary also makes it possible for a small group of older women to go to college part time. About thirty such students leaven the classroom atmosphere. Without any fanfare, the Rosary nuns have thereby aligned themselves with the educational innovation of letting the housewife continue her education. The group includes a few doctors' wives and the wife of a local Congregationalist minister. One suburban housewife has been studying part time at Rosary for twenty years. She took courses because she was interested in them as well as courses for a bachelor's degree. She is now working on a master's degree in library science. The latter program, begun as an undergraduate program in 1930, now graduates about forty every year with master's degrees. More than one-third of the librarians in the Chicago area are graduates of this program.

Modern language training at Rosary not only attracts many undergraduates, but it has given rise to a summer Language Institute for high school teachers. In the summer of 1962, 80 teachers attended. These specialized elements at Rosary, when combined with the fact that a large number of public school teachers in the area graduated from the College, indicate the impact one women's college of quality can have on its surrounding area. Sister Aurelia, Rosary's thoughtful president, enunciates the significance of this impact: "The Catholic college for women which can successfully integrate the universal truths of Catholic thought with the contemporary expansion of knowledge will make a unique contribution toward bringing about a Christian renewal in our complex pluralistic society."

Because of its location in one of Chicago's fanciest suburbs and because it was one of the first colleges to sponsor a junior year of study abroad, Rosary has been mislabeled in the past as a fashionable school for "fancy

work and Bible." The student profile tells an opposite
story. The school's doors are open wide to girls from
all social levels and only slightly ajar for high school
graduates not in the top two-fifths of their classes. Fifty-
nine percent of the 1961 freshman class were in the top
one-fifth of their high school classes and another 27
percent were in the top two-fifths. With about 85 percent
of the students earning part of their college costs in part-
time and summer jobs and more than a third earning all
costs, the students praise the lack of campus snobbish-
ness. One junior said: "I know that at some colleges the
teachers and the students single out girls whose fathers
are rich and important. There is none of that here at
Rosary."

Rosary's tuition is modest, $600 a year, and even the
boarders pay only $1,400 for their entire year's room,
board and tuition. The school estimates another $350 for
books and personal expenses for the boarders. As a group,
95 percent of the students are Catholics, and the bulk
come from the Greater Chicago area, though a small
minority come from outside the Middle West. More
than 30 states and ten foreign countries are represented
at the school.

The Rosary nuns operate a pay-as-you-go enterprise,
never spending more than they take in. The Sinsinawa
Dominicans pay for the sisters' education, a sizable contribution reflected in the number of graduate degrees.
(The sisters point out the variety of universities attended,
especially secular and foreign universities.) There are
more than 30 Ph.D.'s on the faculty, and practically all

the rest have master's degrees, many of them en route to Ph.D.'s.

The biggest contribution is the teaching services of the nuns which amount to 43 percent of the cost of educating each student. The students pay for 51 percent of the cost while the remaining 6 percent comes from miscellaneous sources. The college built up its only endowment of note by the piggy-bank method: each year forfeited room deposits were accumulated and supplemented by small amounts from the college budget. It now has reached almost half a million dollars, fortified a few years ago by a quarter million from the Ford Foundation.

Since 1948, Rosary has been operating the Pius XII Institute in Florence, Italy, for graduate study in fine arts and awarding master's degrees to qualified American students. The Institute is housed in the magnificent Villa Schifanoia, donated by Myron C. Taylor who was President Truman's personal Vatican representative. The following year, the master's program in library science was inaugurated. These moves, along with the junior year program operating since 1925 in Fribourg, Switzerland, blend into the Rosary style: close contact with the world of books, fine arts, and European culture.

The Rosary nuns are convinced that they are neither unrealistic nor impractical in educating young ladies. They point out that a liberal education is the most flexible and the most adaptable for a career or marriage. A specialized education becomes outdated very rapidly, especially for young women who will work only a few years before and possibly after marriage, then think of returning to work when their children grow up. They need general principles, internal resources, and both the aptitude and appetite for continuous learning. For those wanting to specialize, graduate school is the most suitable place, and for the large majority who will soon marry, the Rosary education will serve them well. For their goal of responsible Christians "fully aware and appreciative of the spiritual and cultural heritage of their civilization and nation," the Sinsinawa Dominicans stand by what they consider practical means to realistic academic ends—a liberal arts education.

ST. JOHN'S, COLLEGEVILLE

Living Life Whole

B ETWEEN the Sagata-
gan and the Watab, two obscure and idyllic lakes 80
miles northwest of Minneapolis, a very special college
has been huddled for about 100 years against the side of
a Benedictine monastery. Grouped around the Main
Quadrangle, as if Indians were still in the 2,000 wooded
acres of campus, is the largest Benedictine monastery in
the world, probably the country's most revolutionary
example of Catholic church architecture, and one of
America's most "completely-on-campus" boarding colleges.

At St. John's University in Collegeville, Minnesota,
these are shocking superlatives, for nothing can make

a Benedictine frown faster than a reference to St. John's as a special place. As the leading historian on campus noted: "The Benedictines shrink from institutional pride." While the monks are imbued with this spirit of humility, which is stressed to the "twelfth degree" in St. Benedict's Rule, the college students, lay faculty and alumni can't be restrained. They are uninhibited and vocal in their conviction that there is no college in the country like St. John's.

Certainly, there are other first-rate liberal arts colleges, but few, if any, where life is lived so whole, from the aroma of freshly baked monastery bread seeping into a class on thermodynamics to the family style of learning, playing and worshiping. Isolated, self-contained, situated in an area reputed to have the largest proportion of practicing Catholics in the country, St. John's is ruled by a tradition fourteen centuries old and dominated by the spirit of the Catholic liturgy. Each St. John's day is marked off by group participation in the liturgy, each session enriched by its liturgical adornment. Nevertheless, the mood is modern, and the scene dominated by a daring new church designed by Marcel Breuer, the world-famous architect who executed the UNESCO building at Paris.

When Breuer was selected by the monks to be their architect, St. John's Abbot Baldwin Dworschak said that a principal characteristic of his work was "the undisguised use of basic materials: stone, glass, concrete, wood, brick. His personal simplicity, combined with his zeal for achieving the best possible results, recommended him in every way to the monastic community of St. John's."

The minutes of the April 21, 1953, meeting in which a majority of the monks voted for Breuer describe the architect as "a man of recognized ability, unassuming, direct, easy to work with and yet not afraid to tell you when he thinks you are wrong. His quiet and humble manner, and his willingness to tell exactly what he thinks are the characteristics most in his favor." The monks were obviously using a Benedictine mirror to catch the image of the architect; it was a case of unconscious self-identification in what they saw.

The Johnnies, as the college's students are called, tend to accept membership in the St. John's family as a life-time affair. Some never leave this home. Arriving as students in the residential prep school, they go on to the college, leave for graduate study and then eagerly accept a chance to join the faculty, usually at less salary than they could get elsewhere. In some instances, the college pays the way of a promising graduate at Yale or Harvard so he can come back to teach with a prestigious Ph.D. About half of the 35 laymen on the faculty are St. John's products, though the others become so thoroughly absorbed that it is difficult to tell them apart.

The Benedictines, of course, are the main source of continuity. The overwhelming majority of the 75 Benedictine Fathers on the faculty graduated from the college. The abbot of the monastery entered as a prep school freshman at the age of fourteen; the president, a local farm boy, started in the college. Father Walter Reger, the alumni secretary who is often called "Mr. St. John's," has been there since 1908. When ground was broken in 1949 for a house of studies for diocesan seminarians studying alongside the Benedictines in St. John's School of Divinity, a major seminary, Abbot Alcuin Deutsch summed up the Benedictine commitment to a specific location: "We Benedictines differ from other Orders in that we may be said to belong more permanently to the place where we settle than other Orders. This monastery is the home of its members. We do not belong to a province, but to an independent monastery modelled on the family pattern, and rooted in the surrounding community more deeply and permanently than other religious."

The all-male family at St. John's includes 1,160 college students who live on campus, and 140 day students residing within 25 miles. Also living in are 170 seminarians at the School of Divinity and 320 prep students. The abbey's 90 Benedictine priests in residence are part of a total monastery membership of 254 priests, 57 clerics and 67 brothers. The absent members are on assignment in parish churches or in missions in Mexico, Puerto Rico, Kentucky, the Bahamas, and Japan.

No doubt, the college has its prodigal sons, but its typical product is an average citizen with a sense of social responsibility and a strong Catholic commitment shaped by the sense of belonging experienced at St. John's. After living at a college where his life has been so unified and where he has counted as an individual, a Johnny has the community habit; he relates easily to his community and to his parish, though he is more doer than joiner, more likely to set an example than beat a drum. While the St. John's man is not likely to become rich or famous, one example does personify the St. John's type nationally. He is Eugene McCarthy, former faculty member and now the Democratic Senator from Minnesota, who projects an image of intelligence, idealism and social responsibility. Of course, not everyone at the College, particularly in its conservative economics department, would agree with him politically.

In reflecting on the special quality of St. John's, Professor William L. Cofell, who has specialized in education and psychology and is close to the students as both teacher and counselor, notes, "Speaking from experience, the one very noticeable thing that is learned during an educational experience at a Benedictine institution is the development within oneself of a love and respect for fellow men."

The Benedictines consciously set the style. They offer education with a very personal touch, standing side by side with the students, but avoiding the impression that they are always looking over their shoulders. Father Walter Reger cites the "freedom from subjection to arbitrary authority—authority used selfishly or unreasonably or for ulterior motives." In a thoughtful article on the Benedictine style in education, he stresses three characteristics: "(1) a profound and more than ordinary respect for the freedom of the person, (2) the family principle in our community life, and (3) a strong sacramental spirituality."

Appropriately, Father Walter's alumni popularity stems from his days as prefect, a policeman's job at other colleges. At St. John's, the prefect is a Benedictine everyman—priest, monk, friend, advisor, living example, teacher and taskmaster—and the embodiment of the St.

John's approach. From the prefect's room on every dormitory floor emanates the campus spirit; between one monk and 50 to 100 students in his charge a unique personal relationship develops from partnership in the dual Benedictine theme of Worship and Work. To devote himself to this partnership, the monk-prefect is freed from some duties so that he shares his life with the students, from bowling on their team in the intramural league to leading them in prayers at the end of the day. At the crucial periods during the school year when students receive their academic grades, they receive them personally from the hand of their prefect.

One prefect, in recalling a Christmas party held by his students, provided a glimpse of the Benedictine technique. With a case of Seven-Up on hand, his students were going from room to room singing and enjoying collegiate horseplay, while in the prefect's room several students were busy entertaining him with stories and jokes. At first, the prefect thought the extra attention was in the spirit of the season, until he realized that he was being kept busy while the boys next door "strengthened" the drinks. But for the special occasion, the prefect winked at the infraction "as long as no one got out of hand." He was being unmistakably Benedictine: the spirit of the law outweighed the letter. The prefect could have cited the common-sense advice in Chapter 40 of the original Rule of St. Benedict: "We read, it is true, that wine is by no means a drink for monks; but since the monks of our day cannot be persuaded of this, let us at least agree to drink sparingly and not to satiety, because 'wine makes even the wise fall away.' "

For at least two reasons, living with a monastic prefect requires a considerable adjustment for many St. John's students. About 45 percent come from secular schools where they had no contact with religious; even for the others, living with monks is a far cry from being taught by nuns or brothers. For students coming from mother-dominated homes where the father is diverted from family by the pressures of earning a living, the adjustment has an additional dimension. A student advisor commented: "For possibly 30 to 40 percent of the students, the prefect provides the first consistent contact with male authority; the prefect assumes a father role."

Besides his prefect, each student has a personal advisor from the lay or religious faculty. Also available are the chaplains, the Dean of Men, professional counselors on campus and any faculty member at almost any time at all. Faculty office hours in which students have specified periods for consulting their professors do not fit the Benedictine system. Several lay professors live on campus and all a student has to do is knock on any door. For the family man living off campus or the Benedictines in the monastery, it takes only a phone call to arrange a meeting.

From intramural sports to participation in the liturgy, the St. John's life is enclosed by its family framework. Just as students have both spiritual and intellectual guidance at their doorstep, they are likely to play tennis with a Benedictine, cheer him on in the bowling league or sit next to him in the university orchestra. At one orchestra rehearsal, two Benedictines were found among the first violins, three among the violas, one on the flute, while lay faculty members turned up on the bassoon and the horn. A seminarian was puffing on the oboe as a prep school student created a fuss in percussion.

It's inevitable that the campus atmosphere is casual, Midwestern and rural. One professor pointed to a dent in his rear fender and said: "Deer!" He was referring to the deer that roam the state reserve surrounding the campus; students on a deer-counting march through the woods turned up 125 neighboring deer. Until 1958, St. John's had its own herd of cattle, but the business office pointed to the red ink on the dairy ledger and the aesthetes held their noses, so they were auctioned off. The barn is now a workshop for stained glass where laymen can be seen practicing their craft with a radio blaring out rock 'n' roll music in the background. Campus traditionalists bemoan the loss of the herd, pointing out it is not like St. John's to worry about money or the smell of the farm.

Only in the rural bliss of St. John's could a pacifist lay professor confound the payroll department by refusing to accept more than $600 salary so he wouldn't be subject to income taxes that would be used for military spending. He finally yielded, accepted his salary and then donated most of it to charity. Since he is single and receives free room and board on campus, $600 covers his personal expenses. More typical faculty attitudes range from the family man who teaches at St. John's because "I like this atmosphere and want to raise my kids in it" to the bachelor who points out, "I have all the advantages and none of the disadvantages of the monks."

For the students, the simple life at St. John's is varied

by hitchhiking to town, cars being limited by school regulations to second-semester juniors who are on the honor roll and to seniors. The main supply of dates is at nearby St. Benedict College which is run by Benedictine Sisters. Since the Bennies, as the girls are called, must get back by midnight on Friday, the Johnnies have just time for a movie or dancing on the sawdust-covered floors of a few primitive night spots nearby. On weekend evenings a pair of Benedictine monks makes the rounds of these places to check on the students. The monks are an incongruous sight to the outsider, but the students seem to enjoy their visits. There is no resentment, no awkwardness at the sight of the M.P. monks' patrol, nothing comes to a stop at their appearance, the sound of rock 'n' roll does not die away. The mood of camaraderie is easy, relaxed, and Benedictine.

On campus, dress is about as casual as on the area farms where many students spent their childhood. The college chaplain in his otherwise persuasive weekly letter settles for good dress on Sundays: "Specifically, the school regulations require that on Sundays for Mass you wear a suit with shirt and tie or sport shirt with sport coat, etc. The regulations go on to say that this stupendous degree of well-dressedness be maintained till after the noon meal." For good grooming, the boys rely on student barbers in the dorms who cut hair for 75 cents, half the professional rate locally.

Well over half the college students come from Minnesota, fully in the tradition of a school chartered March 6, 1857, so "that the youths of this new but flourishing territory be not only instructed in the elementary sci-

ences, but, moreover, be educated in sound moral principles." Now that St. John's reputation reaches far from
the shores of the Sagatagan, the students come from
about thirty states and a variety of foreign places like
Germany, Chile, Hungary, Israel, Puerto Rico, Peru
and the Netherlands Antilles.

With its roots in the early history of Minnesota, St.
John's is the oldest Catholic college in the state and the
only college or university in continuous operation in the
state for one hundred years. In his history of St. John's,
Father Colman Barry refers to the fact that in the school's
early years the two major American Catholic immigrant
groups of the period, the Germans and the Irish, "began
to learn to live together and to respect each other's heritage in the melting pot of their frontier school." St.
Patrick's Day is still the occasion for a friendly renewal
of the rivalry between the two groups, featuring a
basketball game and a tug of war between the Irish and
the Germans. (The Irish won both events when I visited
the campus.)

As might be expected, even the admissions procedure
at St. John's has an individual touch. Some way is usually
found to accommodate a deserving applicant with money
problems or to accept the son of a faithful alumnus,
though his marks could be better. About one out of
three students gets financial assistance from the college.
An estimated 35 percent of the student body would be
able to get into any college in the country, while most
are conscientious, average students. Of those who fail,
practically all suffer from lack of motivation, rather
than ability, a study by the college showed. If a high

school graduate finishes in the top 50 percent of his high school class and works hard in college, he is regarded as likely to survive academically.

To offer additional stimulation for superior students, St. John's started an Honors Program in 1958 to supplement the regular curriculum. Beginning with sophomore year, specially selected students do extra reading, take part in seminars and in senior year prepare and defend an Honors thesis. The range of authors covered in this program includes John Dewey and St. Thomas, Riesman, Veblen and Lippmann, as well as Dostoyevsky, Dante and Koestler, Toynbee as well as St. Augustine. The aim of the Honors Program is to "develop a superior student well rounded intellectually and socially, not a bookworm. The Honors student, it is hoped, will be equally at ease in a library, a museum, and at a social gathering." The motivation of students in the program is illustrated by two Honors students who in high school traveled to St. Paul with empty suitcases every weekend from their small home town 50 miles away. They returned home with suitcases filled with books available only in the city's library.

For the average student, adjustment to the self-contained life at St. John's and performance up to its academic standards take their toll, especially during freshman year. One hundred of the 380 freshmen who entered in September, 1959, were gone by the following September. Twenty-four failed; the rest dropped out. The 297 sophomores of that September dropped to 230 by junior year; the 224 juniors became 200 seniors. One student advisor noted that some were preprofessional students leaving for professional training, but two predominating factors were undoubtedly at work: the St. John's family requires adjustment to a tight little island of campus life and St. John's college demands academic performance. Those who graduate merge successfully the stress on belonging and the demands of scholastic achievement; the result is a St. John's man.

The quality of education is reflected in a study of the 1955, 1956 and 1957 graduates by the sociology department. Forty-five percent went to graduate school and if the seminarians are included, the total is 63 percent. An informal report on the football team, an unlikely incubator for graduate students, shows that seven of the 11 starters in 1959 went to graduate school. One faculty fan said of football, the Number One sport: "Sure, the school is out to get good football players, if they are model young men, honor students, sons of prominent alumni and, incidentally, know how to tackle."

Of the college majors ranging from philosophy, history and English through the natural and social sciences to fine arts, the most popular is economics or its variation, economics and business. Father Martin Schirber, head of the economics department and a Harvard Ph.D., makes it clear that the school's liberal arts emphasis is not strained to a breaking point by training average young men for the business world. He emphasizes that there is no "inherent incompatibility between acquiring a marketable skill in college and learning to think clearly and objectively and appreciate deeply." Some of his students are aiming at research and graduate work, others at a postcollege job, and his department in characteristic St.

John's style "has taken a special interest in equipping the average student for intelligent participation in the political, cultural, and economic life of his community."

Theology courses, often a source of student complaints on other Catholic campuses, are well received at St. John's. The emphasis is on understanding the Catholic religion rather than on rote learning, on toleration rather than on apologetics. "Contemporary Protestant Theology" is particularly popular; it is described this way in the college catalog: "The teaching and practice of the Protestant Churches of the United States, with special emphasis on the major bodies: Baptists, Methodists, Lutherans, Episcopalians, Presbyterians. The historical background and foundation of the various groups; the Ecumenical movement; Protestant relations with the Catholic Church. Writings of various contemporary Protestant theologians." One of St. John's brightest students described the spirit of the course in biblical terms of toleration, "From the outset the course sets a theme of toleration, of 'letting both grow up until the harvest.' The course takes Protestant theology at face value. An example of a remark made in class is that John Calvin is undoubtedly a saint."

Characteristically, St. John's was host to a precedent-making colloquy between United States Catholic and Protestant leaders in December, 1960. Papers were presented first on "The Issues That Divide Us" and then on "The Factors That Unite Us." Each session was begun with a Catholic-Protestant recitation of the "Our Father"; each paper was followed by a joint discussion. Some forty years ago, St. John's played a dominant role in

launching the United States liturgical movement, which
centered about one of its most famous monks, Dom
Virgil Michel. The monastery's celebrated Liturgical
Press has exercised wide influence with its publications
as the movement has spread throughout the country. At
St. John's, the movement, with its emphasis on participation in public worship by the congregation, reinforces
the college's family spirit.

St. John's has always been obsessed with maintaining
its self-enclosed environment. Abbot Alcuin Deutsch,
who directed the monastery and college from 1921 until
1950, warned of the "dictatorship of agencies," never
pursued accreditation for St. John's and was wary of expansion. Finally, in 1948, the college applied for and received, in the following year, accreditation from the
North Central Association of Colleges and Secondary
Schools. Abbot Alcuin waited until the last minute before accepting a federal barracks building to house 180
World War II veterans accepted by the registrar. He
relented at 1 P.M. on a crucial Friday, three hours before
the offer expired. He later said that it was the most difficult decision he ever made—to expand St. John's. In recalling that decision, Father Arno Gustin, president of
the college and a knowledgeable educator, notes that the
decision had a condition attached: "If we find that expansion endangers the essence of St. John's, then we will
stop expanding."

The current generation of Johnnies is concerned about
this danger; they are afraid that the St. John's family is
getting too large. The 457 freshmen who enrolled in

September, 1960, comprised the largest class in history and was as large as the entire student body in 1939. Recalling his prewar days as a student, a faculty member described a campus where he knew every other student in the school, where there was one model-T among all the students, a thriving herd of cattle, some stray deer, hardly any lay professors and not a female secretary in sight. Now there are about a dozen secretaries, many cars, no cattle, and a student doesn't know all the students in his own year.

Within recent years, there have been other changes. The honor system has been dropped, ending student courts for penalizing infractions of the rules. The family style of eating at tables served by waiters has been replaced by the cafeteria line. Under the pressure of administrative duties, the abbot had to relinquish his position as college president, becoming chancellor in 1958, and Father Gustin was appointed president. Even this necessary change jarred the family sensitivity of the students, who wanted the abbot's father role in the monastery to be directly applied to the college as well.

While St. John's ratio of two priests for every layman on the faculty is one of the highest in the Catholic field, the growing importance of the lay faculty has probably been the most significant change on campus. It is bound to increase to meet further academic needs. In 1954, there were only five laymen on the faculty; in 1960, thirty; in 1962, thirty-five. In another breakthrough, Professor Edward Henry, who returned to his alma mater to teach political science after completing his doctorate at Harvard, was named assistant to the college president. Still very new on campus, the lay-religious partnership is in an early period of mutual adjustment.

A monastery college poses special problems of administration, especially when the spirit is Benedictine. The order is so thoroughly democratic that all major decisions must be voted on by the entire community of monks; sometimes it is necessary to draw the line between democracy and anarchy. Because the abbot fills a father role for the entire community, there is a temptation to sidetrack the chain of command and to challenge administrative decisions by going directly to him. Moreover, the Benedictine type is less likely to have the attributes of the decision maker and the driving administrator. As a member of a lifelong family, the monk is inclined to avoid friction and to stick to his last. One knowledgeable view of the college's future was presented in these terms: "With half a dozen more top lay faculty members and a strong administration, St. John's could become the best liberal arts college in the country."

Abbot Baldwin, who is the most important individual at St. John's, discusses the future with well formulated ideas and a determination that the family spirit at St. John's will be maintained. The new building program, he emphasizes, is no flirtation with bigness. "This whole plan," he explains, "is a containment program which permits us to give our present numbers the facilities they need. We don't want at all to give the impression we want to be bigger. We want to be more effective." The abbot looks back with nostalgia upon his days as a prefect with only 13 students on his dormitory floor, and he is determined to maintain the personal touch. "The students come to know how we have put the worship of God first," he said. "They actually see us stop our work and go to church several times a day. Every day, our influence is felt all day long. That is why we must remain close to the students."

Neither can St. John's ignore the realities of a booming college population, particularly in its home state of Minnesota. If St. John's merely continues to take the same share of Minnesota college students, it will add about one thousand students in the next ten years. To ensure maximum contact between Benedictine and Johnny, the number of prefects will be increased, along with the chaplains, counselors and advisors. The lay faculty will continue to be recruited with an eye to the professor who has an impact similar to that of a Benedictine. As the abbot expressed it, St. John's will go out of its way to find and retain the layman who fits the system. Faculty-student meetings are being arranged regularly to talk over problems, while off-campus weekend outings are planned under faculty direction. In the sixties, St. John's is becoming a bigger family living in a larger house, but it is determined to give all the children a sense of belonging, even though they don't know each other's names.

The core of the larger St. John's is the newly completed church, part of a master plan of 19 buildings which will eventually replace 75 percent of the present buildings. It is no less than a hundred-year plan, far-ranging and Benedictine in outlook, for as the abbot said to a *Time* magazine reporter, "After all, what are a few generations to the Benedictines?" Before the church, a new monastery and a new dormitory were built; the latter, constructed with the aid of a government loan, caused a bureaucratic stir in Washington when the monks from Minnesota actually sent back $287,000 in leftover funds. Built from local granite, the same material used in the first St. John's building, the new buildings might be called Benedictine modern, the kind a humble builder with a strong aesthetic sense would erect today for maximum utility and minimum ostentation. Next on the list are a new library and a new science building.

From the time they announced their building plans in the spring of 1954, the St. John's Benedictines were surrounded by superlatives. Architect Breuer's plans were described and praised in fifteen magazines in the United States, France, Italy, Spain, Cuba and Japan. One reviewer wrote: "Here is the most exciting architectural story since the building of the great mediaeval churches in Europe." The editor of *Liturgical Arts* said the church is "truly a milestone in the evolution of the architecture of the Catholic Church in this country."

Msgr. Tracy Ellis, the leading historian of the Catholic Church in America, described the abbey-university church in historical perspective: ". . . we have today the startling and original design of Marcel Breuer which, I think, symbolizes as nothing else I know the modern spirit of St. John's and offers a guarantee that here no slavish adherence to the past will obstruct the path of progress . . . it symbolizes the fact that on this campus the past and the present meet in friendly converse, and that by the mingled contributions of these two streams of thought St. John's teaches to all Americans the lesson of the reconciliation of what is of priceless merit in its ancient heritage with the fresh and imaginative approach that our age brings to all it does."

After the church was consecrated on August 24, 1961, it received recognition both from amateurs and experts. The American Institute of Architects named the church as a recipient of its 1962 Honor Awards, the highest architectural recognition in the country. On weekends during the summer of 1961, from four to six thousand persons visited the building and it is still drawing several hundred a week, though some of the monks now have misgivings about creating what has become one of Minnesota's major tourist attractions.

Some outsiders might say humility, mixed with the architectural brilliance of Breuer, has been carried to an extreme in the startling church structure. A cantilevered concrete slab turned on its end replaces a bell tower, and the baptistry, unlike other churches built today, marks the church entrance. (A return to the "originally correct" church planning.) A wall of modernistic stained glass constitutes the front of the church, while on the inside, light, location and design can bring together a lay congregation of 1,664 and a monastic choir of 284 to worship together as one family.

In trying to describe the mood of the church, a European church art magazine wrote: "The space symbol, which this architecture is, must be experienced. One must be in it, move through it, be enveloped by it and pass from one space to another. It creates an environment, a place at which to live at worship. The character

of this space is now grand and monumental, now close
and intimate. Human nature feels at home here; its best
aspirations and varied moods find their expression."

When the monks of St. John's invited twelve of the
world's leading architects to travel to Collegeville to
talk about building a church, they were surprised to
find that all twelve were interested and all but two were
ready to start for the drafting table. In that invitation, the
abbot's statement recalled to many the spirit of Pope
Urban II, the Benedictine who issued the call for the
First Crusade: "The Benedictine tradition at its best chal-
lenges us to think boldly and to cast our ideals in forms
which will be valid for centuries to come, shaping them
with all the genius of present-day materials and techniques." Clearly, the monks of St. John's want a large
picture window with a broad and commanding view of
the outside world into which they send students of their
own special brand. It is just that the window glass must
have a Benedictine glaze of humility and a one-way view
—looking out.

MARYMOUNT COLLEGE
OF VIRGINIA

An Invitation to Learn

MARY HAD a mediocre high school record. Her principal described her as an "average student," which in the current race for admission to college is damnation with faint praise. Her best subjects were English and history, her worst, mathematics and foreign language; this was reflected in a fair verbal score and a poor mathematics score in the College Board Scholastic Aptitude Test. Mary was rejected by two junior colleges, but a third accepted her on the principal's recommendation that "she is intelligent and capable of doing college work."

The invitation to learn came from Marymount College

of Virginia, opened in 1950 as the only Catholic venture
into higher education in the state. It is also an uncom-
mon enterprise in Catholic higher education, a bona fide
junior college. Of the few Catholic junior colleges, several educate nuns only, others yearn for four-year status,
some are weak academically. Marymount, in Arlington,
Virginia, has its mind made up and its accreditation by
the Southern Association of Colleges and Secondary
Schools well in hand. It is neither a finishing school nor
a pilot project for expansion into a four-year college. As
its president, Mother M. Majella, stresses, Marymount
offers a sound two-year college program "geared to eliminate much of the educational waste that results when a
student for one reason or another has not done her best
in high school and has become accustomed to being a
borderline student."

Mary, who stood on that borderline, graduated from
Marymount in June, 1962, after finally accepting the invitation to learn. Marymount reports that at first she
"was a discontented student, not interested in her courses,
resigned to spending two years in college and then stopping." She barely survived the first year and returned in
September, 1961, to react with antagonism toward a
newly instituted "enriched program for liberal arts students." She complained about the "unreasonable" amount
of reading.

Ordinarily, Mary would never have got into college
and if she had, she would never have graduated. But in
her second year at Marymount she developed a desire
to learn, settled down to hard work and set her sights
on continuing in a four-year college. Making up for lost

time, she averaged B-plus in her courses and, according to one teacher's report, "The change in marks fails to show total change in attitude from antagonistic (at least towards hard work) to enthusiastic. Tendency to talk too much and be a bit opinionated vanished in the course of the year without any loss of interest." The teacher was describing a personal satisfaction that is seldom felt in higher education, transforming the nonlearner to the learner. While teaching is generally honored more than research on the Catholic campus, the professor frequently gets his satisfactions from working with the exceptional student. At Marymount, the average student gets special attention.

Taking its cue from the Oxford tutorial system, Marymount has established an Honors Program whose core is seminar discussions. As far as is known, the program is unique in Catholic higher education, for it has adapted the Honors Program usually reserved for gifted students and applied its format of special reading assignments and discussions to the average student. This is done in small groups under the professor teaching a particular liberal arts course. Impressed with the idea, the United States Office of Education helped finance the experimental study that paved the way for establishment of the program at Marymount in September, 1961.

The program, which aims at fostering both motivation and confidence in the students, has been praised on and off the campus. It provided the spark for changing Mary, class of 1962, and judging from student comment, the program has been the miracle of Marymount. The administration is fond of citing the reactions of educators.

Dr. Richard G. Gettell, president of Mount Holyoke, wrote: "The emphasis which your program places on the development of scholarly interest and your concern with the essential purposes of college are particularly noteworthy." In relating the seminar program to the growing role of the junior college, Miss Margaret Clapp, president of Wellesley, noted: "Also it seems likely that in the next decade many students who are fully qualified for a college like Wellesley will start out by preferring a two-year college. Some of them may find that they wish to continue their studies as a result of the program like yours and insofar as the four-year college can make room for them, I think we should do so."

According to the testimony of an expert observer, Dr. Thomas E. Jones, administrative consultant for the Association of American Colleges: "Among the exciting programs in American higher education is the Marymount College Transfer and Terminal Plan. Here potential transfer students including those with average or borderline College Board scores, are enkindled by lectures, group tutorials, written essays and independent study, and two-year terminal students are prepared for positions such as business and medical secretary-ships, merchandising and laboratory technicians. Both groups are exposed to a liberal arts base, enrolled in courses according to tested ability, and surrounded by a Christian home-like atmosphere."

The learning experience was observable at Marymount at regularly scheduled intervals when small groups of young ladies abandoned their classrooms overlooking the fashionable Washington Golf and Country Club and

headed for an academic "bomb shelter." It was their way
of describing an improvised seminar room that will eventually house library stacks, but for the time being it had
four small tables, folding chairs, antiseptic white walls,
and small windows with no view at all of the college's
converted Virginia estate where Teddy Roosevelt used
to ride horseback. Into the seminar room, the Religious
of the Sacred Heart of Mary have carried their campaign to put the accent on the individual and the stress
on higher achievement by all students, stimulating the
average, the above-average and particularly so-called
"under-achievers" whose performance has not matched
potential.

Mother Majella, the soft-spoken president of Marymount, sounds surprisingly martial when she makes it
clear that "nothing is left undone to reach this goal" of
stimulating students. She is a master innovator surrounded
by examples of her determination. Besides the seminar
program, Marymount has a study-aid program, a reading lab, a language lab, a summer independent study program, an experimental science and mathematics course
and, on the immediate horizon, a "logic lab" that should
make the Marymount girls as difficult to argue with as
they are desirable to date.

However, these educational maneuvers take place in
the obscurity of classrooms. The Marymount campus is
serene. Its façade is a graceful set of six tall white pillars
at the main house of the former estate of Admiral Pres-
ley M. Rixey, President Theodore Roosevelt's surgeon
general. It is now the Administration Building. The view
from the rear reveals a beautiful wooded valley with the

golf course in the foreground. The girls claim its well-to-do patrons turn out in the winter snow with golf balls painted red. Off in the distance there are the landmarks of the nation's capital. At Marymount, even the view is reassuring.

Then there are the students, young ladies from upper-middle-class Catholic families, their fathers—professional men or business executives—able to pay $2,200 a year in basic college expenses, not to mention private art or music lessons, spending money, formal clothes, and the occasional plane ticket for a date at Notre Dame. With this kind of student body, the Marymount nuns have come to expect each freshman to arrive with enough luggage to overtax a dormitory room, though the limit was reached with a young lady from Shaker Heights, Cleveland, who arrived with a six-foot, gold-covered (literally) harp.

The sight of the imposing musical instrument in the tiny Student Council room, which was also crowded with fencing foils and masks, set this writer off on a search for the harpist-student. It ended in a serious conversation with an earnest girl who contradicts—as do her fellow students—the misleading image of proper young ladies dabbling in the social graces for two indifferent years at Marymount. Lisa Houk, a doctor's daughter who has been studying the piano for nine years and the harp for six, practices on the harp every day, developing a considerable talent and pursuing a lifelong ambition. She came to Marymount because she wanted two years at a Catholic college before continuing her musical studies at a professional music school. Sensitive, self-possessed, and conveying a quiet charm, this eighteen-year-old girl and her six-foot harp were at home in Marymount.

The school surprises one. Its setting, the secure social status of its students and its position as a small, expensive junior college for "average" students evokes an impression of a finishing school where Aristotle plays second fiddle to Emily Post. Even the Washington, D.C., press has painted such a picture in a traumatic article that still rankles at Marymount. It is so outdated as a description that the students could rehearse for a college production of the musical comedy, *The Boy Friend*, and sing—without any self-consciousness—the description of "perfect young ladies."

The religious of the Sacred Heart of Mary do tend to specialize in "perfect young ladies," and the Marymount students do have an annual four-day charm institute where the social amenities and the secrets of good grooming are gone over carefully. But the order also has developed an international reputation in education since its founding in 1849 in France. Marymounts in New York, Paris, Rome, Barcelona, London and Los Angeles, among more than one hundred colleges and schools, carry a quality label. The order has brought this prestige into the junior college field in response to the growing need for activity in a neglected area of Catholic higher education.

At Marymount, as in most junior colleges, the curriculum and the students are divided into two main groups, the transfer students who plan further study after graduating from Marymount, and the terminal students who are studying to become office secretaries, medical secretaries, or merchandising trainees. The transfer students include liberal arts majors who want to complete four years of college elsewhere, prenursing students and education students. All Marymount students must take a basic group of courses in English, speech, theology and philosophy. The faculty reports, incidentally, that secretarial and merchandising students more than hold their own in the liberal arts courses and by no means drag down the class level. They are analogous to commerce or business administration students in other colleges; often less qualified academically, they have well formulated vocational goals to motivate them.

The handful of nuns at Marymount concentrate on administration and on maintaining close contact with the students in campus life. A part-time and full-time lay faculty of 40, assisted by three priests and five nuns, handles the teaching. While on the alert for the occasional scholar hidden under mediocre high school grades, the faculty counts its main successes in terms of students who have learned to learn and have become enthusiastic about it. One indication of success is the number of students who go on to four-year colleges and graduate from them. Of the 45 who returned for the reunion of the class of 1961, half were continuing their education, including sixteen in four-year colleges and the rest in nursing school or part-time courses. Out of 87 Marymount graduates who went on to four-year colleges between 1952 and 1958, only four failed. Twenty out of the 30 transfer students enrolled in 1957 received college degrees in 1961 after continuing in four-year institutions.

Without Marymount, few might ever have become college graduates. Failure often would have little to do with ability, as Marymount's "study-aid" program has brought out. Three main problems have been isolated: lack of study skills, lack of goals, and the tendency to freeze during examinations. Marymount offers instructions in techniques of note-taking and reading, personal guidance and group dynamics sessions—useful antidotes, if not cures, for these problems.

The faculty, which seems to relish the pleasures and pains of teaching, has in the past few years recruited colleagues with similar appetites for teaching. For instance, Dr. Max E. Guzikowski, who is on the philosophy faculty at Catholic University, accounts for his part-time presence at Marymount by saying: "The more we can give these students the more they can pass on to the children they will have someday. The great thing about Marymount is the personal contact between teacher and student." An English literature teacher recalled a letter from a former student to illustrate the rewards of teaching: "I received a letter from one girl two years after she had graduated. I had forgotten all about her. She identified herself as one of the 'Incorrigibles'—believe me, she was —and then I remembered her. She said she had watched *Hamlet* on TV the night before, remembered my course, and said she actually understood it!"

Drawing on their experiences at well established colleges and universities, the lay faculty insist that they have not lowered their standards or raised their grading system. Several who teach part time at Marymount are on the faculties of nearby Georgetown and Catholic universities. Under the leadership of Mother Majella, the grade of C—unspectacular, but a thoroughly respectable grade on any campus in the nation—has become king, the grade of F fatal. Dr. Guzikowski pointed out that an A or B in his Marymount courses is just as difficult to earn as in his Catholic University courses. The difference is that there are more C's at Marymount. There are F's, too. Twenty-one of the 180 freshmen who entered in 1960 were dropped from Marymount for academic reasons. The trend in grading is illustrated by the same history course as taught by two different teachers during the 1961–1962 school year. Sixty-five percent of one class got C's, 24 percent B's, and 11 percent D's; there were no A's. This is the new Marymount emphasis. The old tendency toward easier grading is represented by the other course in which 18 percent got A's and 33 percent got B's, while only 30 percent got C's.

Marymount has not succeeded overnight in raising its academic standards. This is reflected in one professor's observation that in the early years of the school some girls were graduating without ever being seen in the library, much less borrowing a book. During these years, there were days when not a single book was borrowed from the college library. According to the librarian, the girls now borrow 60 to 70 books a day—sometimes 100 —a respectable figure for a student body of only 278, including secretarial students.

In a frank comparison of past and present at Marymount, Dr. Elizabeth Bernsten described in a report to the school administration the difference brought about by the enriched program with its "Honors" emphasis for the average student. In previous years she found teaching a cross-section of Marymount students in large lecture courses "to be a discouraging and frustrating struggle against massive apathy and resistance to intellectual effort." Only the response of a handful of students made the effort seem worthwhile; by contrast, she felt that she failed to reach only two students during the 1961–1962 school year. In the previous years, she estimates that only 10 percent of the term papers were up to the levels of other colleges in which she has had experience (Marymount, New York, Hunter, Fordham). "During this past year," she claims, "all but about 10 percent of the term papers submitted measured up to such standards and several would have been creditable performances for senior majors in the social sciences."

Introspective, self-critical, pleased, and, also, relieved by the success of the new program, Marymount reports the following changes on campus, which not only indicate improvement but also a need for it: a changed climate of learning, an interest in scholastic work in general and an industrious attitude, a busy library with respectable numbers even on Saturday nights and Sunday afternoons, student conversations on such subjects as contemporary issues, literary subjects, philosophical ideas, and better preparation of assigned work.

In talking to the Marymount girls, it is evident that none was ever culturally, socially or economically deprived, but many have never been listened to as thinking persons. The borderline students have never taken themselves seriously in school and never expected anyone to be interested in their opinions on serious subjects. Their discovery that they can learn and that someone is interested in listening and helping seems to affect their total personalities. No doubt part of this change results from greater maturity and escape from the never-never land of fashionable high schools. One wonders also: What were the teaching conditions in those high schools? Student questionnaires filled out in the spring of 1962 after the first year of the seminar program reflect the previously untapped will to learn:

I have found that the seminars have helped me a great deal as I feel that I can talk more at ease in a group.

The program has helped me in desiring to give my opinion on the subjects in discussion and contribute my ideas. It has been interesting because I learned how the other girls think, whether I agreed or disagreed with their points of view. My ideas of world situations of today have been broadened by our discussion of them and finding contributing factors from past history.

The problems become real problems rather than something that is just read in a book. It makes one stop and think.

Hearing different views makes one more alert to political and historical issues.

Having small seminars allows the teacher and the students to get to know each other.

The smaller classes give me a more confident feeling.

It has made me think more for myself because of the way the teacher asked us questions. When one sits in class, most people, including myself, leave the answers to other people, but, in seminar, this is not true.

Mother Majella, who notes that "you can do things at a junior college that you can't do at a four-year college," regrets that the role of the junior college is not better understood in Catholic circles. The junior-college movement, which dates back to the early part of the century, has boomed in the postwar period and there are now more than 700 junior colleges in the United States, enrolling more than a million regular and part-time students. Today, one in four students begins higher education in a junior college, and by 1975 the figure is expected to be one out of two. Junior colleges are being called the new "third force" in United States higher education. Yet the Department of Education of the National Catholic Welfare Conference reports that there are only 22 Catholic junior colleges with a total enrollment of 5,100. The Rev. William J. Dunne, S.J., who directs the university and college section of the National Catholic Educational Association, agrees with Mother Majella on the need for Catholic junior colleges. "I think Catholic higher education should give greater attention to junior colleges in certain areas of the country," he says. "The junior college is needed in such areas to give a Catholic education to those who can't afford four years of college. I'm thinking of community junior colleges that should be academic rather than vocational."

However, Marymount is expensive and it serves only a handful of students from its immediate area. Except for 30 commuting students, it is a boarding school, drawing mostly from the Middle Atlantic states. There are also students from the Southern and Southwestern states as well as New England and the Midwest. The overwhelming majority come from Catholic high schools. Nonetheless, it sets a standard of educational activity and innovation that can be applied anywhere, though few junior colleges can have the advantage of such a strategic location.

Besides enabling a high school graduate to find herself despite a mediocre high school record and unimpressive College Board scores, the junior college enables the student to mature in an intimate environment. Moreover, a young woman aiming at only two years of college can still receive a diploma. Marymount's secretarial and merchandising students receive an associate degree in applied science, the others an associate degree in arts. Students preparing for the medical service professions of nursing and dental hygiene can complete their preliminary college requirements as a unit instead of dropping out of a four-year college after two years. Those who want more than a secretarial school can offer also find the junior college a suitable answer, as do students trying to make up their minds about college.

Marymount has not had any trouble selling itself on any of these counts. In 1960, only ten years after the arrival of the first 13 students, 180 freshmen enrolled; there were 500 applications for the September, 1961, freshman class of 158. A newly completed dormitory will enable the college to expand in the next two years to its outside limit of 500 students, including a handful of day students. In the process, the liberal arts enrollment is rising sharply in keeping with the college's program of academic uplift.

In Marymount's tight little world, the girls, who are generally from eighteen to twenty years of age, live and study under the protective care of the nuns. The fiction on the library shelves is screened, the girls are chaperoned on group tours, expelled for drinking on dates, penalized for staying out after midnight and forbidden to smoke, except in the smoke-filled recreation room where the bridge players gather and the noontime mail pickup takes place. The most celebrated act of Lenten discipline on campus is practiced by the young ladies who purposely postpone their mail pickup until 9:30 at night, though judging from the daily letter-opening bedlam this form of self-denial is not widely practiced.

Judging from appearances and the comments of the Marymount students, they are by no means a rebellious group. Politically, they tend to be conservative and Republican; socially, their tastes run to Georgetown men; intellectually, they are unpretentious, attentive and modest. They arrive one September as freshmen and become, in effect, seniors the next year, acquiring a sense of responsibility to Marymount, anxious about being accepted by the four-year colleges to which they have applied or concerned about doing well in their first job.

As the student handbook puts it, "the Marymount student is expected to be a well mannered young lady performing the social graces naturally and with ease . . . to be a Marymount student is to be eager, to be enthusiastic not only for formal education, but for all things that contribute to the development of soul, body and mind." To rally the students around these goals, Marymount has launched a Christian Excellence campaign that culminates each March in a week-long seminar and the awarding of a Christian Excellence Medal. Mrs. Robert F. Kennedy, wife of the Attorney-General, was the first recipient in 1961; Admiral George W. Anderson, Chief of Naval Operations, the second recipient.

As the school year comes to a close, the girls attend their main social event, the formal Magnolia Ball in downtown Washington. It begins with a small formality that reflects the school's individual touch. The young man waits at the foot of the elegant main stairway of the Administration Building, his back to the imposing white pillars, his corsage in hand. Down the stairway sweeps his date, impeccable, graceful, concealing her excitement, and double-checked by the unseen nuns on the second floor. As a faculty member pointed out, this graceful stairway exit has the practical advantage of enabling the nuns to take a last-minute look at their young ladies. It sums up Marymount: style, a touch of elegance, a sense of personal responsibility on the part of the faculty, and painstaking preparation of Catholic young ladies.

MARILLAC COLLEGE

Only Nuns Need Apply

THE AMERICAN NUN
has tended to be an outsider on the Catholic campus.
In college she is surrounded by lay students (in sister
parlance, "seculars") and invariably pursues her degree
piecemeal. Isolated on her island of study, she often re-
ceives special care or is merely tolerated, a reduced-rate
undergraduate whose mother superior stands over her
shoulder waiting impatiently for the results. During the
regular school year, the sister-student might be seen in
the back of the room, taking the best notes in the class.
In summer sessions flocks of sisters appear at registration
time, catalogs in hand, their sights on six more credits
toward a degree.

About thirty years ago, one sister, who was indignant at "either being overprotected or ignored," began a program of study that led eventually to a Ph.D. thesis embodying a dream—a special college for nuns only. A realist would have relegated the thesis to the obscurity of a card catalog in a teachers college. A traditionalist would have sensed overtones of feminism, a challenge to the stereotyped passive role of women in religious habits. There is a refreshing directness in the way this particular nun, Sister Bertrande Meyers, discusses the training of women religious, and she does so publicly. In the August 18, 1961, issue of a Catholic newspaper in St. Louis, she made her point by noting that parents "may have a daughter as talented, gifted, devout and as eager to serve as is their son. She enters a religious order, becomes a postulant for six months or a year, is a novice for one or two years, and then lo, she is out teaching fourth grade in a parochial school!

"How has she been formed as a well integrated religious woman in so short a time, and is she professionally prepared as a teacher? The answer is simple. She is not. Yet she, too, is dedicating her entire life to God as a sister under the authority of a religious superior.

"Even the most secular of persons, parents and friends concede that just as a priest is different from laymen, so, too, sisters are different from laywomen. Just as a priest's intellectual studies must be firmly integrated with his spiritual and apostolic studies, so, too, must a sister be formed as a whole person, intellectually, spiritually, socially for community living, and professionally."

In summarizing the goals of the growing interest in

the education of nuns, Sister Bertrande speaks as commander-in-chief of a West Point for nuns. It is called
Marillac College (pronounced Maryac) and it is the realization of her dream college, a school of, by, and for
nuns only. The 350 young women on this unique Catholic campus come from a cross-section of 25 different religious orders, 31 states and a few foreign countries.
Their teachers come from 15 different orders; only one
laywoman, who teaches nursing, is involved in the academic operation.

Marillac, located in the St. Louis suburb of Normandy,
is a shiny, streamlined $5.5-million institution in the middle of an 180-acre estate, a college for women like any
other, except that it is dressed in nun's clothes. Just off
Natural Bridge Road, which leads to the St. Louis airport, a winding rural road turns sharply and leads to its
doorstep. It is an immediate confrontation with what
may be the most daringly designed library on any Catholic campus: four glass walls slanting inward like playing
cards resting on their sides, an improbable sight in unlikely surroundings.

At Marillac, the college is compared to the service
academies where future admirals and generals receive
an education that integrates the intellectual, social and
professional. Instead of patriotism as the fundamental
guiding principle, Marillac, of course, employs religious
ideals and spiritual commitment. Actually, Marillac is
at the forefront of the nationwide Sister Formation
Movement that developed in the early 1950's following
Vatican exhortations that religious orders "provide a
complete formation for their members, from the reli-

gious, apostolic, and professional point of view." When
the Daughters of Charity of St. Vincent de Paul opened
Marillac in 1955, they went one step further, opening
their door to other religious orders as well as to their own
members. Marillac embodies two innovations: an all-sister college environment and a decision to have young
religious earn their bachelor's degrees before taking up
any assignments.

Almost overnight, Marillac received its prized accreditation with highest commendation from the North Central Association of Secondary Schools and Colleges. This
is the same accreditation accorded undergraduate studies
of St. Louis University or the University of Chicago.
After the first Marillac class graduated in 1959, Cardinal
Valerio, Prefect of the Sacred Congregation for Religious, let the school know that Rome was watching and
applauding. In a special letter of praise, he wrote: "Any
initiative that is directed toward assuring for young Religious, even of divers Communities, a milieu reserved ex-
clusively to them and where their religious and professional formation are made into an integrated whole, is
particularly pleasing to this Sacred Congregation."

Marillac, aware that there are still educational skeptics
with a wait-and-see attitude toward its controlled environment, displays testimonials like a first-grader bringing home a report card. Sister Bertrande herself remarks
that it will be ten years "before we know the success of
this experiment." The words are cautious, but the Marillac spirit is filled with faith, hope and unshakeable confidence in the experiment of cooperation by several religious orders in a college education tailormade for nuns.

In a campus conversation almost like any other, the
personal dimensions of Marillac were explored by the
school president, an editor of the school paper and some
honor students. They chatted about campus life, each a
college girl with different background, personality and
interests. It could have been Marymount, Misericordia
or Saint Mary-of-the Woods, except that the students
were all young religious. The straightforward, uninhibited remarks of these young ladies who knew what
they were about is the most authoritative account of the
Marillac experience:

"I attended a girls' college as a religious for two years
before coming here. As to having all nuns in the school,
I just love the idea myself. In classes we all have the
same aim and the same purposes and we're all going to
face the same problems. The teachers can integrate everything and use examples from the religious life. At the
same time, we are not so insulated that we don't know
what's going on in the outside world. . . ."

"I don't have sister's experience to compare with another college, but I appreciate Marillac for the same reason. Here we all can freely discuss things that we know
are common to our lives. It's a tremendous benefit because we can make everything we learn practical right
away. . . ."

"You feel freer to ask questions than if you were in
a college with lay people where you would be careful
about the questions you ask, because they would be interested in what a religious would say and do. . . ."

"I can draw from experience in summer school where
we were together with laymen and women from all dif-

ferent walks of life. As religious, we didn't exactly fit there. The teachers, though they were priests, geared their courses to the seculars in the college. Here, we are getting the fourfold objective of the college—apostolic, intellectual, social and spiritual, all integrated into a whole. . . ."

"Before joining the order, I was a coed in a secular college. But the objectives here are so different. Here, we go to form the entire person; there, I was going for a vocational and intellectual pursuit. Here, when you have sisters that come from all over you take from all and give to all. There, the sisters would not take part in student activities. . . ."

"It seems to me that the big point here is that there is no separation between our intellectual and spiritual life. . . ."

"I think that many of the lay people we might go to school with in secular colleges don't believe that we are exactly human. They look on us as something apart. We are apart in the sense that we have dedicated our lives to God, but we are also women. The difference, I think, lies in the intensity of our dedication. God calls each one in a different way and he calls laywomen in another way. . . . I think that in the training here a sister gets her bearings and her equilibrium. Once she gets her liberal arts education here, she can go out to a secular university easily and be able to stand her ground. Whereas if she goes right away as a young sister, she is not established in her principles and values. To her, the world is still divided between the convent and the seculars, the worldly and the unworldly. Once she is formed, the sister will be able to stand her ground and give the example she should give."

The students and practically all the faculty are enthusiastic about Marillac's prevailing principle that nuns are best served by a special college environment integrating their spiritual, intellectual, social and apostolic formation. This was explained with psychological overtones and a slight Southern accent one Indian summer afternoon in the faculty wing of offices. A psychiatric nurse from New Orleans, who is now a Daughter of Charity and assistant professor of nursing education, explained what the Marillac environment means to a young lady who only recently left behind powder and paint, high heels and Saturday dates.

"The far-reaching advantage here is that the young sister learns first to share with other religious; then she can learn to share with lay people," she said. "After a sister achieves security in her own religious group, she is then more secure in secondary groups. A nun had a concept of herself as a lay person and then adds the concept of herself as a nun. The young nun must converge both into her new 'I am.'"

After stressing that Marillac is an ideal place for discovering the new "I am," she cited two characteristics repeatedly noted by the faculty. The students have boundless motivation and they respond enthusiastically to class discussions in their nuns' environment. Freed from the inhibitions of a mixed environment, they discuss sensitive questions of interest to them as young religious.

The questions range from "Does being a sister make a difference in handling hospital patients?" to "Why do religious become mentally ill?"

Lying on the desk as we talked was an assignment just turned in by a student who went on a practice nursing assignment to a home for the aged. It began: "When I entered Mrs. G.'s room, she was lying down with the blanket pulled over her shoulders as if she were cold. She smiled sweetly at me, and returned my 'Good morning, Mrs. G. How are you? Do you remember who I am?' with 'Good morning. I sure do! You're Sister M. C. How are you?' (My greeting, as I can see now, was not the best, for it directed attention to myself. The aged like to have some attention shown them.)"

Professional in tone and self-critical, the student report catalogued a learning experience which would be subjected to free-wheeling criticism in class. It is a learning situation which a young nun probably would not experience in a class with lay students. Drawing on her experience elsewhere, the nursing teacher noted that her classes carry on spirited critical discussions of student work that would—in a mixed group—reduce a student to tears. The sister-students don't have such a problem at Marillac. They are at home.

The Marillac students are undoubtedly more polite, more chauvinistic about their college and more highly committed than students in other women's colleges. They are continually reminded that they are in a special place and they wholeheartedly agree. At the same time, they carry on such typical campus activities as intramural sports and student elections, hold their regular meetings of Choral, German and French clubs. As one faculty member remarked, "We have practically everything but athletic scholarships." The students refer to the fact that they are not innocent bystanders as they would be in a college with lay students. They become student officers, perform in plays and run the school newspapers, including the nun-photographer who leaps forward camera in hand and startles visiting lecturers with "Hold it. Just one more."

Mock elections were held at presidential time (Kennedy defeated Nixon, 126 to 73), and in an annual Thanksgiving basketball game, the senior class plays the juniors. When the "North" played softball against the "South" on the Fourth of July, the latter won a double-header with at least four casualties caused by overenthusiasm. Mishaps included a collision between a catcher and pitcher pursuing a fly ball and a fractured ankle by a nun sliding into first base. Before you can comment on all these aspects of college life, you are confronted with the rhetorical question: "Would a nun ever become school president in another college?" Then it dawns on you that you never thought a nun would even be interested.

According to the college newspaper, which reflects student exuberance, "A Marillac student has the energy of IBM, the perseverance of a mosquito, the curiosity of a psychiatrist, the neatness of a pin, and the speed of a jet as she goes from one class to another in a single minute." A Daughter of Charity teaching sociology was more restrained, describing Marillac students as typical American girls with middle-class backgrounds. They display a realistic sense and avoid oversimplifying their approach to life. They retain their individual interests and personality and don't aspire to fit into any stereotyped version of a nun.

A July, 1961, survey of 150 Daughters of Charity at the college showed how deeply American their roots are. Slightly more than half had grandparents on both sides of the family who were born in America; only 15 percent had three or four grandparents who were born abroad. Over 60 percent were either the youngest or oldest child in the family: 43 percent were the oldest, 20 percent the youngest. Over two-thirds had gone to Catholic elementary and high schools. Thirty-nine percent decided on a religious vocation after high school and another 28 percent decided in the senior year of high school.

Overall, the students come from 31 states, as well as India, Puerto Rico and Holland, while the faculty has earned degrees from a total of 50 different colleges and universities, antidotes to inbreeding and insularity. Nonetheless, the bulk of the student body and faculty is composed of Daughters of Charity. A total of 240 out of the 350 students are Daughters of Charity, as are 27 out of the 44 faculty members. Eventually, Marillac thinks of expanding in slow stages to 1,000 students.

Inside the streamlined Marillac classrooms, the students have the benefit of an unusual teacher-student ratio, an average of one teacher for every eight students. In one sophomore class on the History of Ideas, the professor faced seven students clustered up front. On the bulletin board, the tone was set by signs containing quotations from St. Thomas Aquinas: "With wisdom man learns from the only Teacher who really knows everything." "Man has an intense desire to know and learn everything but it's neither possible nor convenient."

At one point, the students discussed the question, "What does it mean to be an individual?" The answers mixed the naïveté of college sophomores answering out of their personal experience with references to the intellectual history they were studying. What was different was a velvet politeness which would make the fanciest finishing school look vulgar, not the usual atmosphere in which intellectual dissent is voiced.

However, a Marillac sociology professor warned against regarding such politeness as an automatic roadblock to academic give-and-take. The young nuns apparently have evolved an indirect technique of carrying on discussions. Sometimes the question will be direct— even to the matter of the blunt biological facts discussed in the Old Testament. Often, it will take the path of roundabout statements by one nun with another's followup: "What sister meant was. . . ." Clearly, the good sisters are walking the boundary line between obedience and intellectual subservience. The faculty insists that it fights against the latter successfully. The characteristic Marillac discussion may tend to beat around the bush in its form, but the faculty, conscious of the separation between religious pulpit and academic podium, stress intellectual self-expression and exercise of the student's mind.

In the sober atmosphere, there is less frivolity than in other college environments, fewer distractions and the smile is more in fashion than the giggle or the horse laugh. Nor is there any collegiate concern with being clever or full of repartee. It is likely that no one in the History of Ideas class batted an eye at the typographical slip in the mimeographed course outline which listed Freud's theory under the heading, "Freudalism." (My copy was corrected in ink.)

In the classroom, the sister-students are heard from as students, escaping the two academic extremes which Sister Bertrande condemns in a nun's education: being overprotected or ignored. As the bulletin of the Sister Formation Movement said in a report on Marillac: "With these open young minds in their classes, the Marillac professors find no call for the misguided kindness that has often led directors and teachers of Sisters' summer sessions to make things just a little easier for 'the poor Sisters.'" Sister Bertrande is vocal on the point, criticizing any tendency of a nun to use her habit as a crutch or to hide behind it. "It isn't what I wear but what I do that merits respect," she says and adds for emphasis, "No sister goes out of here until she has earned her degree."

Sister Bertrande likes to emphasize academic standards periodically from the stage of the school's streamlined auditorium. The setting is striking. The soaring starched bonnets of the Daughters of Charity stand out like exclamation points among the two dozen varieties of habits. Though the "bonnets," as they are nicknamed, predominate, the "veils" range from the Glenmary and Ursuline Sisters to Sisters of Christian Charity, Divine Providence, St. Joseph, St. Augustine and the Franciscan Sisters of Our Lady of Perpetual Help. As Sister Bertrande talks, a visitor can't help but notice the shocking pink drapes that frame the stage against a backdrop of sea-green curtains. Her academic emancipation proclamation is heard in a number of statements: "If we run around collecting opinions that agree with us, we will be entrenched in our own ignorance . . . the essence of scholarship is to keep our minds open to new truths . . . no scholarly person closes her mind to other viewpoints . . . being a saint doesn't necessarily guarantee St. Theresa's scholarly work . . . as long as the Church is indifferent or silent, we can hold any opinions we want."

Both faculty and students at Marillac, in striving to keep up with the outside world and to lead a full collegiate life, are acutely aware of the fact that the Achilles' heel of Marillac is isolation and insulation. The students are continually dispatched to St. Louis and its environs via the "yellow peril" (the school bus that keeps breaking down) or "Moby Dick" (the bus that looks and acts like a white whale). Besides their practice teaching and nursing in the surrounding schools and institutions, the nuns are to be seen in the course of the school year at the city's art museum or its sewage or pasteurization plants, the Missouri Historical Museum or the office of Goodwill Industries.

Onto the campus, Sister Bertrande has brought a variety of voices and subjects for the student body as a whole. The news analyst of Station KMOX, the chief of clinical psychiatry at Evansville State Hospital, Slavic dancers, symphonic trios, literary and scientific figures, all have been there. The student body has heard lectures on Communism, science, the humanities, even a special

series of lectures on comparative religion that covered
Judaism, Lutheranism, Anglicanism, Presbyterianism, the
Methodists and the Baptists. A member of an accreditation committee, who reported to Sister Bertrande that he
had stopped two or three sisters at random and asked
them about the Reformation, said in amazement, "I am
a Reformed Lutheran and I can tell you that the description of the Reformation that they gave me is one that
would do my own Reformed Lutheran minister credit."

One supporting piece of evidence for the school's academic standards is the performance of alumnae in graduate school. So far, the number of graduates is small: 36
in both 1959 and 1960, slightly more than 50 in 1961
and 1962. But a random hunt through school files turned
up respectable sets of grades in various academic fields.
An English major collected six B's and two A's at Loyola;
a sociology major, one B-minus, four A-minuses and
four A's at Loyola; a psychology major, two B's and
four A's at Marquette; a biology major, one B, two B-
pluses and seven A's at Fordham. Then there was the
chemistry major at DePaul. She collected 14 straight
A's. One indication of Marillac's impact is the rise in vocations in the St. Louis Province since the college has
gained prominence. Instead of 25 annually, vocations to
the Daughters of Charity have increased to 75 in the
past two years, while dropouts have declined.

With a view to the threefold activities of nuns in teaching, nursing and social service, the academic program
follows the traditional formula of major and minor fields
of study with a liberal arts base. The B.A. is awarded in
history and English, while the B.S. is awarded for majors

in biology, chemistry, physics, natural science, mathematics, psychology, sociology and nursing. Nuns intending to teach take education as a minor field of study. Theology is the North Star for the entire curriculum; as stressed by the college catalog, theology and philosophy are "the strong undergirding for the sister's total formation, emphasizing theology as the unifying principle and the most potent means of integrating all the other elements of her formation." For the Daughters of Charity, Marillac offers a five-year program with the Novitiate year coming after freshman year; nuns from other orders join the college program in sophomore year after completing their first year of college elsewhere. They are not charged for fees, tuition or books.

At Marillac, the students maintain a rigorous schedule. Rising time is 5 A.M. (occasionally, the students report, there is a "late sleep" until 5:50 A.M.) and the crowded day continues until lights out at 9:30 P.M. Classes run from 8 A.M. until noon and from 3 to 5 P.M. The three hours between noon and three are given over to recreation and the various religious rules of 25 orders of nuns. The Daughters of Charity live in the three residence halls on campus, while those from other orders live nearby, some in their motherhouses, others in juniorates. This keeps them in touch with the spirit and practices of their own communities while they participate in the Marillac program. The college's location is particularly strategic because it is in the heart of the "Sister Belt." More than 200 motherhouses controlling the activities of half of the nation's 170,000 nuns are located in eighteen Midwestern states.

Marillac, as part of the Sister Formation Movement, has significance for a gigantic Catholic enterprise involving nearly 5 million primary school students and practically a million on the secondary level, an educational system largely in the hands of teaching sisters. As summed up by a Catholic publication, "Stated simply, Sister Formation is a nationwide campaign to make Sisters more saintly, skilled and mature, and thereby more efficient in the face of ever greater demands on the Church unaccompanied by a commensurate increase in vocations." In its specific application, Sister Formation is bound to vary with time, place, conditions and the 377 communities of sisters in the United States.

With its emergence as a fully accredited nuns' college that is a melting pot of various religious orders both on the learning and teaching end, Marillac has naturally attracted attention as an approach to Sister Formation. But despite Sister Bertrande's vigorous leadership and the dynamic atmosphere at Marillac, not everyone is convinced that its controlled environment is the best means of sister formation. Even a few Marillac faculty members from other orders have reservations, though they maintain a discreet silence on campus. Some educators in the area share the reservations about the academic isolation of the nuns, though they indicate with admiration that one should never underestimate the power of a nun, especially Sister Bertrande. As president, she dominates to such an extent that it is difficult to separate the Marillac formula from its combination formulator-activator-innovator.

A sister prominent in Catholic education summed up

the feelings about the Marillac "experiment" among the unconvinced. While there is agreement on the merits of keeping young religious separate during their first two years of college, she argued that the competition of lay students and the stimulation of a variety of professors are vital in junior and senior years. In her experience, classes containing all sisters are invariably "more passive" than mixed classes, and young sisters who go into teaching assignments before finishing college mature more rapidly than those who remain four consecutive years. "I am suspicious," she said, "of incubators that turn out nuns all the same way." She also observed that an operation like Marillac (which has a high ratio of Ph.D.'s and a well qualified faculty culled from various orders) may ultimately face a dilemma: to siphon off much needed professors or to settle for second-best.

Sister Bertrande, with considerable merit and support, rejects out-of-hand charges that Marillac is "raising hothouse plants" or "spoon-feeding" young religious. Moreover, she points out that Marillac's role is confined to the undergraduate level, preparing young sisters for a mixed environment after graduation. The Marillac charter was revised so it could never become an all-sister university. The debate continues, but the spirit behind the emergence of the American nun as a forceful participant is clearly set down by the executive secretary of the Sister Formation Conference, Sister Annette Walters: "Sisters will not be able to fulfill the mission which the Church confides in them unless they are educated in such a way as to play leadership roles in their association with adults."

Certainly, as far as its students are concerned, there is no place like Marillac. As they look ahead to graduation, the sister-students display the school loyalty of a West Point cadet or a Notre Dame freshman after a winning football season. A faculty member might note that there are other colleges where nuns are being successfully trained, but the students, especially the seniors, are not impressed. In conversation, the seniors look ahead with a mixture of impatience and hesitation, pride and humility, sharing the sense of opportunity and responsibility of all college graduates: "If you go on to graduate work the standards are so high at Marillac that you really fit in. The sisters who have gone to graduate school have come back and told us this. . . ." "I know I am going to make a lot of mistakes, but I feel that at least I am ready to start, that I have a lot behind me. I am looking forward to it. Well, I feel like a little potato getting out of the oven. . . ." "We go out of Marillac with gratitude and love and hope that we will do what we are supposed to do and prove that these years have not been wasted. I think there is eagerness. We want to get out and put all this to work. . . ." "People expect so much of you when they know you are from Marillac. It's going to be a bigger challenge."

ROSARY HILL

The Creation of a College

IMMEDIATELY after World War II, as colleges opened their doors wide to returning veterans, a nun in Western New York realized that the doors would not be so wide nor the classrooms so large as to accommodate all qualified young women in pursuit of a degree. Sister Mary Antoinette, then in her seventies and still active as supervisor of sister education, urged her superiors in the Sisters of St. Francis of Penance and Christian Charity to accommodate a growing demand by founding a women's college. Therein begins the postwar tale of the creation of Rosary Hill College, in its way an adventure story filled with near misses, chance-taking, heroines, a happy ending, and an uncertain opening chapter.

The story is set in Buffalo, Western New York's largest city, a sober, steadfast, orderly community where the Sisters of St. Francis had distinguished themselves in elementary and secondary education. But their only venture beyond that was a small normal school where the order trained its own members to become teachers; they had no other American experience in higher education. There was little cash on hand for a college, just the money-borrowing proclivities of an international order described by one of its Rosary Hill members as "always in debt." Moreover, Buffalo already had the well established D'Youville College where the Grey Nuns of the Sacred Heart have been educating young ladies since 1908.

Within their own group, the Franciscan nuns had only a handful of members qualified to teach in a college and they already had their hands full at their ongoing enterprises. There was also some outside skepticism about well meaning nuns who had to have themselves a college, and there was not even a generous benefactor in sight ready to donate one of the many mansions that recall genteel living in Buffalo.

Nonetheless, the Franciscan nuns plunged in. In 1945 and 1946, real estate men in the Buffalo area were confronted by an elderly nun and a vigorous, sharp-eyed companion, Sister M. Gonzaga (now Mother Gonzaga). Object: estate with ample grounds suitable for conversion to a college. Price: reasonable. Payment: some cash down and the rest borrowed from a willing bank. Wherever there was a For Sale sign on a large house with ample grounds, a pair of nuns was likely to be seen, surveying the scene, talking about land values, location, renovation possibilities, and price. The eventual purchase in the northern Buffalo suburb of Snyder was one of those farseeing moves that has made many a real estate manipulator rich. It anticipated the growth of suburbs; the city as well as the students have followed the St. Francis nuns to their twenty-nine acres along the outer reaches of Buffalo's Main Street.

When the nuns hung out their shingle in the summer of 1948, announcing the location of Rosary Hill College, they were surprised at how small the sign and how large the cornfield that obscured the main house and garage of the estate they had purchased from a retired manufacturer of parachutes. This was their college: the cornfield, the main house converted into classrooms and a cafeteria, the servants' quarters that housed the nuns, a small lake renamed Fatima Lake, and the garage that became a science laboratory. Several of the 44 freshmen who arrived in the fall of 1948 had trouble finding the school; it was very easy to drive right by the cornfield that had a sign saying there was a college behind the stalks.

Yet when the indomitable Sister Antoinette died in the spring of 1962 at the age of ninety-two, the very young college was a leading and fully accredited institution of higher learning in Western New York, its cornfield replaced by a rolling lawn crowned by a streamlined complex of classrooms, library and dormitory. It is now impossible for passing motorists to miss the striking $1.3-million classroom-administration-science building called Duns Scotus Hall, the sixth campus addition since

1948 when the nuns bought the estate for $135,000. Still building, Rosary Hill opened Lourdes Hall (addition No. 7) in the fall of 1962, fourteen years after its first 44 students had arrived. The enrollment totaled 700 students, including the 163 boarders in Lourdes Hall; 800, including part-time students. There was no hyperbole in the speech by Monsignor Leo E. Hammerl, superintendent of Buffalo diocesan schools, at the dedication of Lourdes Hall; the Sisters had built a college "from humble beginnings to great stature and significance in the community." The dazzling result in such a short time made what seemed like wild speculation in 1948 look like a conservative blueprint for the future.

As a postwar success story in Catholic higher education, Rosary Hill has many themes, not the least of which is the nuns' faith in Divine Providence. Even those who wouldn't agree with their faith must admit it was a highly functional confidence, which sustained the college from its feeble beginnings. The nuns are fond of noting that the motto of their community is "God Will Provide," but they also point out that it is necessary to cooperate with Divine Providence by rolling up your sleeves and working hard. With a gesture that resembled a right jab, the college's president pointed to her desk and remarked: "God will provide, but nobody except me must clear up that correspondence on my desk." Her name is Sister M. Angela and in a characteristic touch of Franciscan humility she is listed in the back rather than the front of the college catalog, along with the rest of the administration and faculty.

Operationally, Rosary Hill succeeded by turning what

could have been drawbacks into assets. There never have been enough nuns to meet faculty needs, so promising young laymen and women were hired, including the many male professors who give the campus a distinctive male presence often absent in Catholic women's colleges. Lacking experience, the school was not hidebound; it planned its academic program after studying the newest and oldest college operations. Lacking tradition, it gave the students the opportunity to feel they were part of something new and vigorous, an alma mater in the making, not a middle-aged enterprise with a precedent for every problem. Rosary Hill offered a campus but it was also close to home, only a bus ride away for Buffalo-area students. Even the cornfield served its purposes, for it meant that when the time came for expansion there was room to build.

The obvious reason for Rosary Hill's success was the multiplying demand for a college education in the country generally and in Western New York specifically, an area with a preponderance of Catholics. It is what Sister Angela means by her Biblical reference to the birth of the college in "due season." In Rosary Hill's immediate area of Niagara and Erie Counties, 9,000 students graduated from high school in 1959. The New York State Education Department estimates an increase of 140 percent to 22,000 by 1970 when Rosary Hill expects to have a student body of 1,000 at its peak of expansion.

In retrospect, Rosary Hill won a series of calculated gambles based on this supply-and-demand situation in higher education. Although it did not seem that way at the time, the first gamble—founding the college—possibly was the smallest one of all, though the college had to change its name at the last minute and postpone its opening by one year. In their original application for a state charter, the nuns registered as Marian College, but at the last minute state officials notified them that another college application had been submitted under the same name. So over one weekend the nuns had to choose a new name. Rosary was the first choice, but because of Rosary College near Chicago (described elsewhere in this book), Sister Antoinette suggested the adding of Hill. It avoided confusion and was justifiable since the college is located in an area once known as College Hill.

Rosary Hill, formerly Marian and almost Rosary, College planned to start classes in September, 1947. The estate's owner, George Waite, was ready to complete the sale as soon as he found a new home in the South where he planned to move for his health. But he was not well enough either to move or to look for a new home so the nuns had to wait or find another suitable estate. Suddenly Mr. Waite died in December, 1947, the deal was finally closed in late spring, and the Franciscan nuns moved in on July 22, 1948, only two months before classes started.

Buffalo took little notice of Rosary Hill's first year except for a few newspaper articles, including one about the College's performance of *Romeo and Juliet*. Aside from any dramatic merit, the production was noteworthy because the cast was composed of the entire student body. In those days, the nuns walked around their estate figuring out how they would build and expand; there was no lack of confidence, just of students, faculty,

and money. They had 44 students and a faculty of six
sisters, one priest, and three part-time lay instructors.

Then three parallel processes were set in motion. The
College increased in both students and faculty; buildings
were added; and the nuns begged, borrowed and raised
money. Before the first year was over, a music wing was
added to the science laboratory which had once been a
garage. In January, 1950, when enrollment reached 126,
the first floor of Daeman Hall was opened; the second
story was added in 1952 when there were about 200
students. Daeman now contains music studios and the
Little Theatre whose seats were bought when the Er-
langer, Buffalo's last legitimate theater, closed.

Mother M. Alphonse, who died in 1953, guided Rosary
Hill during its formative years as its first president and
prepared the College for the great leap forward it made
under her successor, Sister Angela. In awarding her an
honorary doctorate in 1960, St. John's University in
Brooklyn summed up Sister Angela's role as builder and
expander: "Under her inspired leadership, Rosary Hill
College received Middle States accreditation, tripled its
enrollment, almost doubled its faculty, and expanded
physically and academically so that her achievement may
be considered phenomenal."

Marian Library, which was completed in time for the
1955–1956 school year, was followed by one strategic
real estate move and two calculated risks. The real estate
involved an adjacent four-acre estate which the nuns
had counted on buying in order to round out their
campus. Suddenly they learned it had been sold to
someone else, despite their hopes, expectations and pray-

ers. Sister Angela recalls sprinkling the area with holy
water and stringing up Franciscan rosary beads (which
have seven decades) on a neighboring tree, and praying.
There was nothing else to do. The mansion had been
sold as the new location of a downtown synagogue.
Then just as suddenly, Sister Angela got a call inform-
ing her that fine print in the zoning regulations had nulli-
fied the sale. The fine print said, "for residence only."
Within ten days, Rosary Hill had bought the estate, and
not too soon at that. For within a month, a state court
invalidated such zoning restrictions in regard to houses
of worship. The estate became Alverno Hall, the school's
first dormitory, and in the fall of 1956 the first 40 boarders carried their luggage onto the campus and the enrollment approached 300. With a gift of another adjoin-
ing estate from its Advisory Board, the College reached
its present physical size of 29 acres, becoming Buffalo's
convenient campus for Catholic college girls.

The College had space, but not enough of a roof. It
needed classrooms, offices, laboratories. The obvious answer was Duns Scotus Hall, but the question was how
much of an answer at how high an investment. Some
downtown Buffalo friends counseled the nuns against
plunging too deeply. One friendly priest warned the
nuns against letting department heads outline their needs
in the new building; their eyes would be bigger than the
College's pocketbook. And what if enrollment did not
expand enough to fill the new classrooms?

Not surprisingly, the nuns went ahead and were
proved right. They built their $1.3-million four-story

metal and glass-walled building of contemporary design, floating a substantial bank loan. On September 20, 1959, Duns Scotus Hall was dedicated to the Immaculate Conception and named after the Franciscan theologian and philosopher who argued for the doctrine in the fourteenth century. And enrollment continued to rise: 500 in the fall of 1959 and 600 the following year, not including part-time students. Lourdes Hall, the next major move, depended on attracting a substantial number of resident students, especially since a million-dollar federal loan had to be financed. When it was dedicated on September 30, 1961, every room was filled and its residents included girls from 52 cities and towns in New York State. Through it all, the cost of an education at Rosary Hill has not soared. A day student pays tuition of $700 and a general all-inclusive fee of $100. Room and board costs $850 to $900.

Duns Scotus and Lourdes halls are the first parts of an $8-million development program to move off the drawing board. By 1972, the College plans to have a new fine arts building that will include an auditorium, another student residence hall, a new faculty residence, an addition to Duns Scotus and a new student chapel. Also included in the plans are funds for faculty raises and pensions, library books and scholarships. Brother Cajetan J. B. Baumann, O.F.M., a leading Catholic architect, has also included a tall, slender carillon in the master plan he has drawn up for the college. It is his trademark, but, as Sister Angela is quick to add, Rosary Hill's expansion has been markedly functional. The carillon will be the last and only decorative investment. "It's a long way off," she said. "If bell ringing is necessary, I shall go out and ring a hand bell myself."

Rosary Hill also has had to work hard on image-building, another formidable and unavoidable pressure in higher education. As a newcomer, it had to run twice as fast, join twice as many organizations, attend conferences and meetings twice as often. Besides accreditation by the Board of Regents of New York State and the Middle States Association of Colleges and Secondary Schools, Rosary Hill is affiliated with The Catholic University of America. These steps are standard among Catholic colleges, but add, also, membership in a total of 17 organizations for a college only fifteen years old. Reporting on conference-going from college president on down, a single issue of the faculty bulletin listed the following organizations whose meetings were attended by Rosary Hill representatives: Association of Colleges and Universities, Registrars and Financial Aid Officers, American Alumni Council, Washington Conference on Federal Government Programs for Colleges and Universities, North East Conference on the Teaching of Foreign Languages, Catholic Economic Association, American Economic Association, American Association for the Advancement of Science. In the summer of 1962 the college sent two nuns to Oxford, one to Paris, others to Oak Ridge (Tennessee), Wisconsin and Oklahoma.

Although long-range plans call for a faculty half lay and half religious, the lay faculty, particularly the men, predominate. The faculty and part- and full-time instruction is composed of 18 nuns, four priests, and 39 lay members—29 of them men. The overhead involved in such a lay faculty means considerable pressure on the college budget, yet the nuns have not been guilty of shortchanging on salary. The pay scale is comparable with those of other private colleges and the administration is outspoken about its intention to pay to keep a valuable faculty member. Professor John T. Masterson, who has taught at Rosary Hill from the beginning and who married one of his former students, illustrates the way the nuns have distributed authority between lay and religious. As head of the English concentration (equivalent to a department), Professor Masterson has jurisdiction over the dean of students and the academic dean, who teach English courses part time. They conscientiously clear with him on what they do as English teachers; the positions are reversed when he deals with them as deans.

Having recruited such a high proportion of male professors, the nuns have faced the fact that they must treat them as professionals, leaving choice of textbooks and content of courses to them and their department heads. Generally young and committed to lifetime careers in teaching, the lay faculty members can be seen sitting at two long tables in a plain dining room into which they carry their lunches from the student cafeteria. The mood there is informal, animated and intimate, and the conversation ranges from students to politics and philosophy, from golf matches to baby-sitting problems. In frank discussions, the Rosary Hill faculty did not sound like housebroken teachers at a nuns' college for girls.

It's a faculty that does more than teach and run. It

spends a great deal of time on campus and in various activities. Faculty members even take turns writing essays in *The Ascent*, the school newspaper. Characteristic of the newspaper's efforts to extend its vision beyond the campus was an enterprising student article titled, "Anatomy of a John Birch Meeting." Reading in a Buffalo newspaper that the John Birch Society had not invaded Buffalo, the girls knew this wasn't so and arranged to attend and describe a local meeting. In another school, the published article might have been ringing with partisanship on one side or the other. In *The Ascent* it was a measured, chronological report in which the last paragraph stood out: "At an informal gathering after the [John Birch Society] meeting one member made this observation concerning his membership in the controversial group: 'I can't understand it. I was a normal human being before I joined the Society; now people look at me as if I had sprouted horns.' "

In one of the faculty essays in the college newspaper, Mr. William O. Kerr, a young philosophy instructor who insists on pointing out to students that his field is truth-seeking not dogma, considered the difference between Catholic and non-Catholic colleges. His was the sound of the new generation of lay professors heard on various Catholic campuses, young men and women defining their multiple role as teachers, intellectuals, and Catholics. The Rosary Hill environment appears to be hospitable to what he feels and thinks: "The important difference, which does not necessitate special objects of study, is that Catholic educators must have a unique fearlessness about the pursuit of truths. They believe, or ought to, that true faith is completed and enhanced by the freedom of scientific and critical research, in which no genius is overlooked for purely religious reasons. It is this freedom of faith which gives meaning to 'Catholic college' and to the notion that 'The Truth shall make you free.' A faith which is afraid of defeat is no faith at all, and the absence of such fear ideally expresses the core meaning of 'Catholic' in 'Catholic colleges.' "

During the spring, 1962, term, two philosophy professors joined by English and history professors debated two controversial issues: resumption of nuclear testing and United States support of the United Nations. With the Student Association Assembly as their audience, the four men dramatized the liberal and conservative viewpoints within the faculty itself. This faculty debate was echoed in each issue of the school newspaper with opposing columns presenting student views of liberalism and conservatism. (Such dialogues on public issues are disappointingly absent from many Catholic college newspapers.) A newly formed Pen and Quill study group attracted student attention at about the same time with a series of discussions led by various faculty members. The series covered C. P. Snow, Arthur Miller's *The Crucible*, Morris West's *Daughter of Silence* and that universal campus favorite, *Catcher in the Rye*. No doubt, it was just coincidence that the director of freshmen, Sister M. Cletus, led the discussion of J. D. Salinger's touching story of adolescent growing pains. The discussion brought out student consensus that Salinger's rough language was a necessary part of the characterization. As a campus best-seller, *Catcher in the Rye* was joined by *Tender Is the Night* and *To Kill a Mockingbird*.

The nuns at Rosary Hill are soft-sell educators. Their tone is Franciscan, informal, friendly, intimate and good-natured. While they have the situation well in hand, they are not overly authoritarian; they have the knack of providing the small personal touch and of projecting humility. The Student Handbook claims that the college "is noted for its warm, friendly attitude . . . a visitor to the college will note the friendly student-faculty relationship." Though student handbooks are to be read more for stated ideals than for day-to-day realities, this is one claim that can be sensed on the Rosary Hill campus. It's a friendly place. Even the dean of students, often regarded on campuses as a martinet with a book of regulations under her arm and a suspicious look in her eyes, is popular. In 1960, the yearbook was dedicated to Sister Paula—"friend, educator, dean, confidante, idealist, administrator."

Sister Paula's administration of Lourdes Hall, the new dormitory, illustrates her approach as well as Rosary Hill's. The students place themselves on the honor system by signing a pledge "to assume the responsibility" for the honor system. They promise to report themselves for infractions and to ask fellow students to report their own infractions. The student pledge also places a firm hand inside the velvet glove, concluding with the line, "If she refuses to do so [report herself], I will report her to one of the four Resident Council officers." If the girls stay out beyond the curfew, they are expected to penalize themselves the next time by coming in that much earlier. Even the ban on drinking has a human touch: "No student shall drink alcoholic beverages unless it is a social necessity and never to excess." When the girls were discussing the honor system, they raised the question of how the college would know that a girl is telling the truth if she phoned in at night to report that she would be late because her date's car broke down. Sister Paula's reply: "Now listen, honey, if we have to start calling garages to ask about broken-down cars, then we had better give up the honor system. If you say so, we believe you."

At Lourdes Hall, all the girls take turns waiting on tables and clean their own rooms. To lessen the danger of cliques, the girls nominate themselves in campus elections so that a girl does not have to gather a small army of followers in order to run for office. She is expected to make her own decision on whether she is qualified and able to handle the job. One girl, in trying to recall why she decided to enroll at Rosary Hill, said: "I came to see the school, met Sister Paula, and that made up my mind."

Even Sister Angela, who has her hands full making decisions and directing the college, keeps her door open to students wanting to see her. One junior told of sitting around one evening with her classmates when the conversation got around to campus complaints. Someone said: "We ought to go see Sister Angela." Instead of dropping the suggestion as outlandish, one of the girls made an appointment to see Sister Angela and presented a list of 12 complaints. For two hours, Sister Angela listened and then explained the administration point of

view. Another girl recalled an incident that occurred
during her first week in college. One rainy morning
while rushing from Duns Scotus to another building for
her next class, she practically bowled over a nun walking along the path. Seeing she had no umbrella, the nun
offered the one she was using and insisted when the girl
refused. As the freshman rushed off with the borrowed
umbrella, she suddenly realized she didn't know who
the nun was. She turned and stammered, "Where should
I return the umbrella?" The answer, "Oh, just leave it in
my office." Only later did the freshman discover that she
had the president's umbrella.

The girls are at a loss to explain the friendly campus
atmosphere. They seem to take it for granted and are a
little surprised when asked about it. A few said in almost
identical words: "I know it sounds corny, but the college motto explains it: 'Doing the truth in charity.' " The
nuns pinpoint their approach in terms of development
of the will. Each individual is expected to guide herself
responsibly; conscious wrongdoing is the main concern.
The nuns are sensitive to the dangers of coercion and
rigid supervision which, instead of developing the will,
either suppress it or make it rebellious. One nun defined
the direct command in the way of St. Francis: "If you
wish it, so do I." Another said that the one in power "is
last, least, and lowest; the higher one goes, the more
humble he or she becomes." It is a fragile message that
can't be transmitted in a systematic way, depending instead on the dedication, style and example of those setting
the pace at Rosary Hill—the nuns themselves, seconded
by the lay faculty.

For instance, the president's umbrella story is matched by the example of a senior who was rushing to complete her term project, but interrupted her work to spend a weekend just before the deadline helping a classmate who was further behind than she. During their Christmas and Easter holidays local students take turns caring for the menagerie of mice, rabbits, guinea pigs, parakeets and chickens housed in the biology lab. When the girls complain about such things as not being able to smoke in their rooms, they also add the positive side: there is a lounge for smoking on every floor in the dormitory. The Rosary Hill girls seem to be walking on the sunny side of the street and their trip into womanhood is being done the Franciscan way without conspicuous consumption of spiritual, social or material resources.

The nuns also have a formal description of their educational philosophy. They took pains to summarize it in a catalog of a few years ago, though it has been abbreviated in later editions in keeping with the direct, pithy style of most college catalogs. "The educational plan of Rosary Hill College is based on the seven-hundred-year-old Franciscan concept of knowledge developed by St. Bonaventure," the summary stated. "It recognizes a two-fold purpose in all human pursuits and studies: the repairing of the integrity of human nature and the alleviation of the needs of life. The former is accomplished by securing wisdom through the study of the liberal arts, as well as the practical and speculative sciences, and by repelling vice through the application of religious and moral principles to action, or the practice of virtue. The latter, the alleviation of the needs of life, whether mate-

rial or spiritual, is accomplished through the skills of
vocational arts and, in some cases, acquaintance with the
humanities."

"Repairing of the integrity of human nature" in an
academic curriculum requiring history, science, English
literature and Latin or mathematics as well as philosophy
and theology, not to mention electives, is easier said than
done, especially in an era of academic specialization,
scientific breakthroughs and sociological, political and
economic complexity. But the nuns have tried. Beyond
stating that the "curriculum is determined by philosophy
and integrated by theology," the nuns developed a Coordinating Seminar "to provide an integrating course in
which the student studies the interpenetration of theology and philosophy with her own field, and the inter-
relation of the various fields of knowledge." Once a
month the entire senior class met for a lecture on a field
of knowledge; the other weekly meetings, involving special lecturers and discussion, took place within the students' specialization.

In this instance, there was a slip between the catalog
and the classroom. As one senior faculty member explained: "It is almost impossible to succeed in coordinating all fields of knowledge with theology and philosophy
in the Coordinating Seminar. Where do you find men
who know enough theology and philosophy on one hand
and are specialists in another area as well? At this stage,
we are succeeding in integrating a student's major field
of study, not all fields from biology to sociology." The
nuns feel exposure of the seniors to the latest developments in other fields of study enlarges their horizon;

some of the lay faculty feel such exposure to a little
knowledge is unsatisfactory and might encourage intellectual smugness. While the Coordinating Seminar
aimed at more than it achieved, it is the kind of venture
that is more likely to be found at a new college—a place
that is self-consciously seeking new answers or trying to
adopt established answers. If the nuns have succeeded in
"coordinating" it is not in the letter but in the spirit of
the college.

Aware of the problem, Rosary Hill combined—beginning in the fall of 1962—the Coordinating Seminar
with a Proseminar which gives students a chance to do
independent research. Across the range of academe,
seniors in the spring of 1962 were doing research on
"Paper Chromatography," "Independents of Euclid's
Parallel Postulates," "Social Teaching of Pius XII," "A
Comparison of the First Complete Sonatas of Haydn,
Beethoven and Schubert," "Profit Sharing," "Ultraviolet
Experiments" and "Eugene O'Neill—How His Life Influenced His Plays." Each field of concentration holds a
special session in which seniors sum up the high points of
their research papers before an audience of classmates
and faculty. At the English Proseminar, the girls dis-
played wit, self-confidence, occasional irony, a few
flashes of insight—all the traits of maturity that college
seniors develop. The seniors were involved in a two-sided
cerebral operation: they were taking themselves seriously
intellectually and they were also being taken seriously
by classmates and faculty.

The senior doing the Eugene O'Neill project placed
in unconscious juxtaposition the two most conscious

traits of the Rosary Hill girls. She referred to the fact
that O'Neill's grandfather settled in Buffalo and to the
fact that he was born a Catholic. The Rosary Hill girls
are practically all Catholics, most of them graduates of
private Catholic high schools. Sixty-eight percent are
from the Buffalo area; only 32 out of an enrollment of
660 were from outside New York State.

Undoubtedly the Buffalo mentality is entwined with
the Franciscan style in creating the atmosphere at Rosary
Hill. A conservative city with many immigrant groups,
a stable core of white Protestant families and a population of 1.7 million that is 50 percent Catholic, Buffalo
shuns extremes. Its life revolves around the home, especially during the bitter winter months, and in the pleas-
ant summer months there are beaches, state parks and
golf courses. One of the Rosary Hill students from New
York City referred to Buffalo as a city "where everyone
eats supper at 5 o'clock in the evening." The preponderance of Buffalonians in the student body contributes to
the harmony. Most of the Buffalo girls plan to live, work
and raise a family in their hometown area. They are not
on a collegiate spree far from home; Rosary Hill blends
into their tranquil, secure personal biographies. If a
Rosary Hill graduate moves away, in many cases the
reason will be that her husband's company has assigned
him elsewhere. As a city, Buffalo is large enough to hold
its young, while at the same time retaining a small-town
atmosphere. Accustomed to feeling at home, the students
bring that feeling to the college and develop it there.

Yet there are enough exceptional and ambitious students as well as individualists to create a stimulating mix-

ture at the college. The influx of residential students has helped considerably in this regard. The girls come to Rosary Hill for obvious reasons: its location close to home (the Main Street bus stops at the door); its campus; its position as a first-rate, small, Catholic, girls' college; its Franciscan nuns. These are all reasons cited by the girls who say repeatedly that they picked the college on the enthusiastic testimony of students or alumnae or after visiting the campus and finding it so "friendly" (that word again, unrehearsed, but there).

The English program, which is highly regarded in upstate New York, has attracted many of the students. Sociology, under the direction of Mr. Charles M. Barresi, a young sociologist who is completing his doctorate at the University of Buffalo, has been increasing in popularity. The art department is distinguished by Sister M. Jeanne who made a local television hit as the first nun in the state to teach a college-credit course on open-circuit TV. For girls aiming at a career in the specialized fields of medical technology and medical record librarianship, Rosary Hill has developed programs with strong appeal.

The college is set up along concentrations, which are equivalent to departments as far as the faculty is concerned. But, for the students, this means more work in depth in their major field of study, without a secondary emphasis on a minor field of study. Sister M. Georgia, who remains one of the most popular figures on campus, though she holds the reins as academic dean, did the original homework on planning the curriculum along with Mother Gonzaga. She argues for her program as making for thoroughness and providing a sound preparation for graduate work or jobs immediately. The first two years of study are general, though students make a tentative choice at the beginning of sophomore year when they take a basic course that tests their ability to cope with the concentration they have in mind. In senior year, the seminars are the culmination of the concentration program. However, for the large number of students preparing to teach, the necessary educational courses constitute what amounts to a minor field of study.

Besides fulfilling its original *raison d'être*—college training for qualified high school graduates—Rosary Hill has moved on to the next stage—supplying area schools with teachers and hospitals with medical technicians. From 40 to 50 percent of each graduating class goes into teaching, the overwhelming majority on the high school level, a statistic with considerable impact in Western New York. When part-time study, especially by teachers, is included, about one-third go on to graduate school. As expected, about 60 percent of the 468 who graduated between 1952 and 1961 are married already. The immediate postgraduation biographies of the 73 members of the class of 1961 are typical: 40 percent in high school teaching and 5 percent in elementary schools; 10 percent full time in graduate school, including five with assistantships or fellowships at New York University, Columbia, Syracuse, Fordham and St. John's. The remainder are married and/or working, including several in medical technology.

Probably because Rosary Hill is a new school and therefore introspective, faculty, administration and even students conduct self-analyses and appraisals. The college paper's "Galloping Poll" asked 387 students: "Are education courses necessary?" A total of 269 answered yes, with the freshmen (who have the least experience with education courses) 87 percent in favor. An even split resulted from the question, "Do you believe too great an emphasis is placed on credits and grades in collegiate circles?" But an interesting contrast was evident: 61 percent of the seniors felt that too great an emphasis is placed on grades, while 68 percent of the freshmen had the opposite opinion. The academic dean distributes unsigned questionnaires each fall to the seniors, varying the questions according to the answers needed. Some questions have asked the students to name the most helpful teachers, the most maturing courses. Though the nuns sift student opinion carefully, they do take it seriously.

The most sophisticated attempts at surveying are made each year by sociology seniors under the direction of Professor Barresi. They have probed the image of Rosary Hill in the community and the attitude toward intellectualism on campus. Using a rating scale, the students found that 46 percent of Buffalonians in a professional or managerial class had a good to excellent image of Rosary Hill College, as did 42 percent of the students interviewed in Buffalo. On the other hand, clerical and sales workers, laborers and housewives had poor to fair images of the College. When the girls on campus were rated on their attitude to intellectualism in 1959, they were generally rated as having neither a high nor a low rating; they had a medium rating. The majority of girls said that most Rosary Hill students do discuss their studies outside class, study as hard in electives as in their concentration, but asking if most preferred a lecture date to a movie date was going too far. Only eleven girls would agree that lecture dates are preferred to movies; 87 said movies top lectures on a date. (Canisius students, who are leading collegiate dating material for Rosary Hill, can rest easy.)

At the College's ten-year mark, Miss Joyce Fink, a Rosary Hill alumna who is now assistant to the president, surveyed graduates between 1952 and 1958 and turned up findings that bear out various points already made. Based on a response by 62.4 percent of the alumnae, Miss Fink found that they regarded their college experience as very helpful in preparing them for an occupation, cultural development and enjoyment, and social adaptability. From 64 to 75 percent of the alumnae said Rosary Hill "helped very much" in these areas. However, only 25 percent felt it "helped very much" in civic and community life. More voted for philosophy as very helpful than for theology in coping with everyday problems, while among the few who found neither helpful, six times as many said theology did not help. Forty-two percent went to Rosary Hill because it was nearby, 15 percent because of the influence of friends. Asked to choose the most valuable asset of the college, 39 percent checked off "Franciscan and religious spirit," more than twice the number picking the next choice, the courses offered. Finally, 92 percent said they would pick Rosary Hill if they had it to do over again and 94 percent want their daughters to go there.

The final question to ask at this stage in the remarkable emergence in fifteen years of a first-rate women's college from a cornfield is: Will success spoil Rosary Hill?

Judging from the eternal collegiate triangle of students, faculty and administration, success should improve Rosary Hill. The continuously rising demand for a college education along with the rising image of Rosary Hill means more and better students will apply. From 350 applications for the 1958 freshman class, the total rose to about 600 for the 1962 class, including a much higher number of dormitory applicants than can be accommodated. Thus the quality of dormitory students will probably rise more than the general level. In the freshman class of 1961, the median on verbal scores in the College Boards was 470, a rise of 20 over the previous four years. The 1961 class of 213 freshmen included 22 in the charmed circle of 600 to 700 and 36 with 500 to 550 scores. The college maintains a "rolling admission policy" weighing special talents and particularly high school transcripts which Sister M. Desales, director of admissions, has found to be the best predictor of college performance. As the enrollment rises, the nuns are confident that the Rosary Hill spirit will be transmitted to each group of incoming freshmen by those ahead of them, undiluted by the size of the student body. On the testimony so far, this is how many students recall being infected with the contagious friendliness and harmony.

The faculty has a shortage of Ph.D.'s, the status symbols of the academic world, but several key members are on the verge of completing doctoral dissertations and this will improve the showing on this count. The ad-

ministration, for its part, is certainly devoid of smugness
and there is no reason to doubt that the forward push of
the college will be maintained. Having gone this far, the
nuns are determined to keep going, a determination
epitomized by that remarkable combination of Franciscan humility and ivy-covered expansionism that sits
in the president's chair. Sister Angela points out that she
"uses the Bell Telephone Company" to answer her problems; the answer is as close as a telephone call to someone who knows it, and she is quick to add, "We had to
do in five years what others had 30 years to do." Already
sensing both a trend and a need, she pointed out that the
college has had a lay advisory committee since its beginning and will soon add two laymen to its Board of
Trustees. Also, the lay role in the administration of the
college will be enlarged, while the number of religious
on the faculty will increase. As long as the nuns maintain their flexibility and continue to develop their lay-
religious partnership, the success story should go on.
After all, there is a clear and continuing demand for a
small (comparatively), well rated Catholic women's college in Western New York. And these nuns of St. Francis are indefatigable doers as well as dreamers.

THE CHANGING
CATHOLIC CAMPUS

I N 1937, Robert Hutchins accused Catholic higher education of imitating the worst features of secular education and ignoring most of the good ones. Today, with the widespread burial of football and the self-conscious buildup of academic standards, Catholic colleges and universities are so busy imitating the good features of secular education that they are blurring their identity.

Catholic university presidents, the real and symbolic spokesmen for Catholic higher education, repeatedly confront the elusive problem of defining the present-day role and the character of Catholic colleges and universities. Their answers are not as consistent as might be expected. Sometimes it seems that a Catholic university president, besides all the other appalling qualifications of

office, must have split vision. He looks heavenward when
the audience is Catholic and emphasizes the relation of
the Catholic campus to the salvation of souls. Then he
can point to the special character of the Catholic college
or university. When the audience is non-Catholic, particularly when it includes important members of the
business or academic community, his gaze shifts down-
ward—toward the world around us—and he points to
the university's role as a bearer and giver of knowledge
for its own sake and for the sake of a pluralistic society.
Then he can point out how similar the Catholic university and college are to the rest of higher education.

Father William J. Dunne, S.J., a former college president who is now associate secretary for the College and
University Department of the National Catholic Educational Association, pinpointed the problem at a July,
1961, convention in which he addressed representatives of Catholic institutions on "University Relations
Through the President's Eyes." He raised the issue directly: "In some of your university relations offices the
question is being discussed with regard to the emphasis
to be placed or not to be placed upon the religious nature of our colleges and universities."

At another point in his speech, he said: "We have
been speaking of a certain perplexity over the national
image of Catholic education. It is not altogether surprising, then, to find in these times a kind of 'shying away'
from the religious character of our colleges and universities. You can observe this in many brochures and
publicity pieces. There is an obvious 'playing down' of

the religious side of our institutions. Whether this is done to enlarge the green pastures of the fund raisers or to broaden the field of student recruitment I do not know. Whatever the motives are, I simply say that it is bad."

The situation is paradoxical. While pursuing knowledge for its own sake no matter what the outcome, Catholic schools are also trying to stress a total Catholic framework for the intellectual life. Academic individualists push boldly ahead in their work, confident that truth is unified and that no fundamental contradictions will develop. The more timid, concerned about short-term problems and eager to conform, shy from potentially controversial areas; a number of college administrators favor the timid.

In entering the mainstream of American higher education, Catholic schools are trying to remain both Catholic and American. Sometimes the two seem incompatible. Catholic schools want to keep their individual personalities and their special religious commitment, but they also want to belong, a dilemma that confronted America's immigrant groups. The older generation wants to remember the old country; the new generation is in a hurry to Americanize.

When asked to prepare a considered statement on the present state of Catholic higher education, Father Paul Reinert, S.J., the president of St. Louis University, responded: "Catholic higher education is in a state of reexamination and reevaluation. It is going through a period of preparation for the greatly increased responsibilities of the future. In this period of transition, educators are evaluating the strengths and weaknesses of Catholic higher education to enable them to make judicious decisions about the future."

Father Reinert was talking about a changing Catholic campus, a new personality in the making for Catholic higher education. This was evident in my visits to campuses throughout the country over a period of many months. Perplexity over the image of Catholic higher education was inevitable once the postwar transformation got under way in quantity and quality as well as outlook. As long as the Catholic campus cut itself off from the rest of higher education, its identity was easily preserved. It was isolated, self-centered, limited in quantity, quality and intellectual aspirations, undisturbed by winds of change.

While Catholic higher education has not abandoned the universally accepted definition of its special function, it is attempting to apply the definition in the new and sometimes overwhelming context of expansion, improvement and involvement in the academic mainstream. As set down in the catalog of the oldest Catholic institution of higher learning, Georgetown University, "A special function of the Catholic college is to impart in a thousand ways, which defy formulation, the Catholic attitude toward life as a whole." The products will be "students who are stamped with certain traits which come into play and govern their approach to life in every sphere; students, therefore, who realize that Catholicism is not merely a creed but a culture."

As a miniature community embracing all aspects of a student's life, the Catholic campus readily applies this definition to personal outlook, social experiences and religious involvement. By the mere token of providing a Catholic environment, the campus community is bound to succeed—to some degree, at least—in imparting Catholic culture. But the pursuit of knowledge is still the basic function of a college and many Catholic intellectuals disagree violently with simplified interpretations of the notion expressed in a typical pamphlet answering the question, "Why a Catholic College?": "I can only say, with G. K. Chesterton, that there is a Catholic way of teaching everything, even the alphabet, if only to teach it in such a way that those who learn it won't look down on those who don't." While this attitude, which derives from Cardinal Newman's "The Idea of a University," can be applied literally to elementary and secondary schools, its application on the college and university level, without regard to its subtleties, conflicts with the uninhibited pursuit of knowledge essential to higher education. Aside from the obvious impossibility of Catholicizing such fields as mathematics and engineering, it can lead to academic ghettoes where the young are protected by the timid and the timid are protected by their isolation from the outside world.

However, new ideals are emerging on the Catholic campus. There is more emphasis on loyalty to an academic discipline rather than to preconceived notions or safe opinions. This was epitomized by a priest-professor of comparative religion who said the best compliment he can receive for published articles is that his religious faith is not obvious in what he writes. It is no longer fashionable to overload courses with Catholic authors, books and references that leave the student ignorant of the important work in the field. There are even some who doubt that the thirteenth was the greatest of all centuries and anyone who tries to make Shakespeare into a Catholic is laughed at. Even Protestant theology is being taught, not in order to conduct a mock war in apologetics—with the outcome assured—but to develop intellectual understanding. The focus is shifting from indoctrination to education, though there is no consensus on the magnitude of the shift.

A new intellectual tone is bound to figure prominently in the changing Catholic campus and inevitably it will provoke cases involving academic freedom. In one institution, a leading professor said he had criticized the political actions of the United States hierarchy in his political science class; in another, a non-Catholic English teacher said that when his students ask about books on the Index, he tells them that it is not his concern, that he personally thinks the Index is "nonsense," and that they should consult a priest. In a third institution, a serious case of academic freedom was being thrashed out behind the scenes.

The postwar Catholic faculty, dominated by laymen and fortified by a growing number of secular doctorates among priests and religious as well as laymen, is the agent of change, supported by college and university administrators determined to enter the mainstream of higher education. This determination has encouraged the new generation of lay, clerical and religious faculty, the Americanizers (to repeat the analogy of the immigrants). Professionally, they want to get ahead on their achievements and their abilities. Invariably, they are Ph.D.'s or near-Ph.D.'s who are determined to create an intellectual climate on campus and are openly critical of intellectual dullness. They want their own work and that of their students to stand on a par with that of any American school. This new generation is also demanding that theology and philosophy meet the demanding standards of scholarship and they are gradually raising the academic stature of both fields.

By contrast, examples of the older type linger on, unpublished, with dusty master's degrees and with fading esteem as men who once "fit in" but who now are seldom respected for their learning. They belong to the "old country" of prewar days when character was often built at the expense of the mind, when the Catholic campus could be described as a place where priests tried to act like laymen and laymen tried to act like priests. In their growing obsolescence, these men and women are often figures of pathos, enjoying cold comfort for past commitment and dedicated service. To give their generation its due, many of its members carried on a noteworthy tradition of quality in the classics and the liberal arts, which were a justifiable source of pride on many prewar Catholic campuses.

The Catholic campus has become the laboratory for a lay-clerical partnership vital to Catholic higher education and of significance to American Catholicism. If the partnership cannot succeed in the controlled and favorable atmosphere of an academic community, its chances are remote in the outlying parishes. Unless competent laymen and women are attracted to the Catholic campus at a time when the pursuit of faculty is becoming increasingly competitive, the expansion of Catholic higher education is in jeopardy. Salary is part of the problem, but so are status and position on campus. Writing in the November 10, 1961, issue of *Commonweal*, Father James J. Maguire of Notre Dame's Theology Department stated unequivocally, "Yet there can hardly be any doubt that at this juncture in American Catholic higher education, the prime need is for a sense of genuine academic community that unites religious and layman in a common identification." At present, most laymen on the Catholic campus tend to feel like second-class citizens, though it is fashionable for Catholic college and university officials to proclaim their equality. At least that is a beginning.

While Catholic schools imitate the best qualities of secular schools, the students still seem to reflect the worst qualities of their secular counterparts. The average Catholic college students often appear too concerned with athletics in college and a job after graduation, too little concerned with the issues of the day and the problems of the world. The best Catholic college students are a match for college students anywhere, but the middle group reflects social and economic limitations. It has been said that the Jesuits were sent to America to raise the proletariat to the middle class; to a large extent Catholic higher education is still engaged in this mission. Ironically, many in the prewar generation of successful Catholic college graduates are sending their sons to prestige secular institutions.

As the last to change on the changing Catholic campus, the students still cling to their political indifference, though an unprecedented number of public figures appeared at Catholic schools during the 1960 presidential campaign. Catholic college students tend to repeat the political attitudes of their parents; their Democratic tendencies reflect working-class backgrounds, big-city influences, and the impact of a Catholic President. Nowhere in my travels did the conservative revival seem very strong; there was little passion for politics in the first place. Some observers blamed the indifference partly on the approach of the faculty and the policies of college administrators.

It is more in attitude than ability that Catholic college students seem to differ from their secular counterparts. Organization men are being incubated in large numbers on the Catholic campus, though the spirit of personal service and idealism typified in the Peace Corps is gaining headway. An encouraging sign was the growing interest in serving church and country among the brighter students, with increasing numbers attracted to the teaching profession and an impressive percentage going on to graduate school. Yet, for many, college remains an avenue for social and economic progress. The appetite for learning often seems underdeveloped.

But it is dangerous to generalize about one-third of a million students. Anyone who has been in a class filled with the bright and eager and in a class dominated by the mediocre and indifferent realizes the range of student material being processed by Catholic schools. Moreover, since the majority of living alumni of Catholic colleges and universities belong to the postwar period, their impact as participants in the pluralistic society is not yet clear.

At the present time, the great debate within Catholic higher education involves those who might be described as the idealists and the realists. The idealists, usually dissatisfied with the level of Catholic intellectual life and setting very high goals, speak repeatedly of excellence. From his perch in the public relations center of Catholic higher education, Father Hesburgh of Notre Dame has been the most audible and controversial exponent of excellence. The basic analysis of Catholic intellectual life in America was made in 1955 by Monsignor John Tracy Ellis of Catholic University. It is not a flattering picture and the reaction to it in Catholic circles has not subsided. Monsignor Ellis placed the blame for the "inadequacy of Catholic scholarship" on his coreligionists: "The chief blame, I firmly believe, lies with Catholics themselves. It lies in their frequently self-imposed ghetto mentality which prevents them from mingling as they should with their non-Catholic colleagues, and in their lack of industry and the habits of work, to which Hutchins alluded in 1937."

The view of the "realists" was expressed in the spring of 1962 by Father William F. Kelley, president of Marquette University, who said in a speech in Washington, D.C.: "Personally I am angered by the disservice to Catholic higher education of many in our ranks during the past several decades. The disservice lies in this: that their focus is so fixed on one facet of higher education, namely what they call the production of 'intellectuals,' that there is never sufficient emphasis put on the heroic, gigantic strides taken by Catholic higher education, particularly in the past 30 years." After describing the strides, he made his point: "What I am saying is that there is quite a considerable volume of splendid college education being provided for the preponderance of American young people in institutions that are not primarily research institutes."

On one hand, the call to excellence out of the depths and on the other hand, the hurrah for progress—possibly there is only a difference in theoretical viewpoints, representative of two different attitudes in the field of Catholic higher education. But there also are practical problems. Many Catholic educators are concerned about the proliferation of inferior Catholic schools and the tendency of well established institutions to overextend themselves. One of the latest to speak out was Professor Robert F. Byrnes, in his presidential address at the December, 1961, meeting of the American Catholic Historical Association. "Finally," he said, "I have not noted the large number of third-rate academic institutions, many of them Catholic, which betray our youth and our values and waste our substance. We must somehow put the 'house of intellect' in order by abolishing these discredited institutions."

Among the well established institutions there is a counterpart tendency to branch out into technical and specialized areas where they have neither faculty nor resources to carry on respectable enterprises. Instead of developing a strong regional department on a cooperative basis, individual institutions compete with one another. The result is mediocrity, particularly on the graduate school level where the Catholic record is relatively un-distinguished. What is needed—though few heeded the proposal when it was made by Monsignor Ellis in his controversial 1955 article—is national planning made for Catholic higher education to end its haphazard, laissez-faire development. Unless Catholic schools learn to co-operate and to coordinate their operations, the need for funds and for faculty will overwhelm them. There is danger that a Darwinian struggle for survival will over-take the evolution of the Catholic campus.

Instead of four-year colleges perishing, they should merge with other institutions or be converted into much-needed junior colleges. Second-rate universities should retrench and become first-rate colleges. Universities in the same area should limit themselves to specialties they can handle well on the graduate level and either abandon the others or consolidate such departments with other Catholic universities.

A national planning board for Catholic higher educa-tion would not (and should not) eliminate the mosaic of colleges and universities, each responding to different needs and situations. But the pieces might be made to fit together more effectively while the basic characteristics of these schools with a view remain the same. They are —and will be—Catholic and American.